ART AND REALITY:

Ways of the Creative Process

ART AND REALITY:
Ways of the Creative Process

BY JOYCE CARY

Essay Index Reprint Series

 BOOKS FOR LIBRARIES PRESS
FREEPORT, NEW YORK

Originally published as Volume 20 of the
World Perspectives Series

Reprinted 1970 by arrangement with
Harper & Row, Publishers, Inc.

To

EDITH HAGGARD

INTERNATIONAL STANDARD BOOK NUMBER:

0-8369-1906-8

LIBRARY OF CONGRESS CATALOG CARD NUMBER:

77-128218

PRINTED IN THE UNITED STATES OF AMERICA

CONTENTS

WORLD PERSPECTIVES *What This
Series Means*   ix

PREFACE   xv

I. THE ARTIST AND THE WORLD   1
II. ART AS MEANS   8
III. MIND AND FEELING   13
IV. THE REALM OF PERSONALITY   16
V. WHAT MEN LIVE BY   22
VI. ART AND TRUTH   26
VII. THE REALM OF INTUITION   31
VIII. ORIGINALITY   35
IX. EDUCATION   38
X. VALUE AND MEANING   44
XI. NATIVE GENIUS   50
XII. DEATH OF OLD SYMBOLS   53
XIII. THE MEANING OF THE SYMBOL   57
XIV. DIFFERENCE IN SYMBOLS   62
XV. IMPRESSIONISTS   67
XVI. FORM OF THE SYMBOL   71
XVII. STYLE   74
XVIII. INTUITION AND CONCEPT   79
XIX. EXPLORATION AND CONSTRUCTION   84
XX. EXPRESSION AND COMMUNICATION   88
XXI. EXPERIENCE AND WORD   94

XXII.	THE TOTAL SYMBOL	98
XXIII.	REVOLUTION OF AN IDEOLOGY	104
XXIV.	REVELATION AND ART	106
XXV.	IDEA AND FORM	110
XXVI.	LIMITATIONS OF FORM	115
XXVII.	CREATIVITY AND THE SUBCONSCIOUS	119
XXVIII.	MIND AND EDUCATION	124
XXIX.	LOGIC AND THE SUBCONSCIOUS	128
XXX.	MORAL JUDGMENT	134
XXXI.	GOOD AND EVIL	146
XXXII.	THE MORAL CONSTANT	150
XXXIII.	MEANING AND MORALITY	154
XXXIV.	MEANS AND ENDS	161
XXXV.	THE FORM OF ALLEGORY	166
XXXVI.	POWER OF THE SYMBOL	172

World Perspectives

What This Series Means

WORLD PERSPECTIVES is the expression of a new vision
of reality. It is a program to mark the spiritual and intellectual revolution through which humanity is passing. It
aims to provide an authoritative perspective on the fundamental questions of our modern age, taking into account the
changing cultural, scientific, religious, social, political, economic, and artistic influences upon man's total experience.
It hopes to define through its universal principle and its individual volumes man's greater orientation in the world and
the unprecedented development in men's feeling for nature
and for each other.

Through the creative effort of the most responsible world
leaders in thought, who have a paternity in the new consciousness and in the enlarged conceptual framework of
reference of our epoch, this Series attempts to evoke not a
rebirth of good will but vigorous ideas capable of overcoming
misconceptions and confusing traditions and of restoring
man's faith in his spiritual and moral worth and in his place
in the cosmic scheme.

World Perspectives has been conceived out of a concern for
the overwhelming accretion of facts which natural science has
produced but upon which this science has failed, by virtue

ix

of the inherent limitations of its present methods, to bestow any adequate meaning. It is the thesis of this Series that man has lost himself as the living center in a world created by himself. He has been fragmented into different categories which are the subject matter of various scientific approaches to reality with the result that he has become a heterogeneous mass of isolated pieces of reality, of spheres of objects. And the subjectivity left to him has been either driven into the cognitively irrelevant, remote corner of the emotions or his self has been formalized into the logical subject of scientific analysis, leaving him impotent to grasp the inner synthesis and organic unity of life.

There are, however, manifestations of a slow, if reluctant, awakening, and man as the experiencing, responsible and deciding self, endowed by nature with freedom and will, yet beset with confusion and isolated from the dynamic stream of living reality, begins to recognize the ominous implications of the loss of his center and to see that the different realms of scientific approaches to life, to man in relation to himself and his world, have been falsified. He is increasingly aware that his predicament consists in his inhuman situation of being treated and of treating himself as an object among objects, and as a consequence his image of the unity, order and beauty of the universe has collapsed. It is this new consciousness which *World Perspectives* endeavors to define, and thus hopefully to present a critically examined doctrine of man which may become a healing and preserving force capable of counteracting the apocalyptic era in which we live.

The conceptual framework of man's thinking in the West and in the East, our authors believe, has become inadequate for understanding our world. The models and symbols that have served in the past no longer suffice; the old metaphors have lost their relevance and mankind has been emptied of its spiritual orientation and moral certitude. Our chief anxiety issues not from new experiences but from the fact that space and time, that implicit framework of all experience, have changed. Both actual life and theoretical thinking have out-run our powers of imagination. And yet our imagination is deeply influenced by those scientific notions which our reason is unable to fathom. The theoretical constructions on which the marvels of our world age are erected transcend the very language we speak, for finally they can be expressed only in mathematical symbols.

As space and time have changed their appearance and shat-tered our most elementary foothold in the physical world, and as language itself has undergone a mutation, we have been thrown into a state of anarchy and suspicion, conscious that science which has fathered these changes is itself threat-ened unless it too can be attuned to the wider and deeper range of human thought and human experience. For it ap-pears that unless great spiritual resources are present men tend to lie prostrate, to droop as mere victims of conditions and circumstances.

World Perspectives is born out of this consciousness of man's spiritual poverty and conceptual failure. For now the question of the human meaning of man's knowledge can no longer be repressed. The qualitative uniqueness of every life process and especially the uniqueness of that process which is called human is the subject of scrutiny of this Series. It attempts to point to a dialectic of polarity in which unity and diversity are accepted as simultaneous and necessary aspects of the same essence. It is a protest against that philosophy which neglected the existing man and turned exclusively to the structure of the world. It is an effort to show that not causality alone but relationship as well constitute the living reality. It warns of the tragic implications of the atomization of our knowledge of man and nature which though a matter of expediency is at the same time a cause for distortion. And finally, this Series is a consistent endeavor to contribute to the construction of the new, yet ancient, morality of the new world age in the new world community by analyzing and re-defining not only the traditional and obvious ethical aspects of life but the nature of life itself including the nature of man's relationship to the universe, himself and all mankind. Only through such reflections may those basic concepts emerge which will permit the human spirit to ride disaster and wring victory out of the extremity of defeat, vindicating human freedom and the power of human personality. For finally seminal concepts must replace rampant ideologies.

World Perspectives presents powerful thinkers, unafraid and unimpeded, fiercely and unremittingly dedicated to the universal and unitive meaning of life which may emerge out of the disciplined vision of reality. The authors of this Series endeavor to be the architects of the edifice constituting this new reality through poignant concepts, basic, powerful, novel, in order that the human mind may encompass and control what the human spirit may envisage and what human hands may touch. Implicit in this Series is the commitment to new ideas which come only through the quiet dissolving of prejudices, through the influence of new conditions that give birth to new prepossessions, through a certain necessary oblivion in the handling of tradition from one generation to another and through a process of elision by which mankind can surrender to novel and enlarged points of view without knowing it.

The authors of *World Perspectives* attempt to articulate the deep changes in men's minds that cannot be reached by logical argument, for it is a mysterious virtue in the nature of man that he is capable of working for purposes greater than those of which he may be conscious and greater than any act of volition he may make, however mighty; as though there were an invisible creative force at work in the universe, subtle and inexplicable, in the midst of confusion.

In this way, it is submitted, *World Perspectives* attempts to show that man is that unique organism in terms of matter and energy, space and time, which is urged to conscious purpose through reason, his distinguishing principle. In this way the parochial society of the past may be ultimately transformed into the universal society of the future. In this way man may be unlocked from systems of thought which imprison and destroy. And this may be achieved only if the human heart and mind remember that principle of life, that law of the universe, that dynamic process and structure affording man a rocklike foundation while engendering the maximum elasticity of his intellect. And this principle, this law, remains now as ever before: Hold to the truth, to the unity and continuity of man and the unity and continuity of knowledge, to the unmediated wholeness of feeling and thought, the unity of the knower and the known, of the outer and inner, of subject and object, particle and wave, form and matter, self and not-self. As to the fragmented remainder, let us be totally uncommitted while we explore, enrich and advance the unfolding of the life process which relentlessly presses forward to actualize new forms.

RUTH NANDA ANSHEN

New York, 1958

PREFACE

I HAVE to thank the Master and Council of Trinity College, Cambridge, for the invitation to give the six Clark Lectures, and Professor F. P. Wilson of Oxford for commissioning the course of three at Oxford in Hilary Term, 1952, on *The Novel as Truth*, and so obliging me to examine my ideas on the whole subject.

I am grateful to Mr Robert Ogilvie of Clare College, Cambridge, for reading the Clark Lectures in my enforced absence.

In the preparation of a reading text from scattered notes, my secretary, Miss Edith Millen, showed her invariable patience, accuracy and understanding of the matter; and this version for the book owes everything to the critical eye of my friend, Mrs Dan Davin, who has worked with me over every page.

J. C.

OXFORD
March 1957

THE ARTIST AND THE WORLD

THIS is an attempt to examine the relation of the artist with the world as it seems to him, and to see what he does with it. That is to say, on the one side with what is called the artist's intuition, on the other with his production, or the work of art.

My only title to discuss the matter is some practical knowledge of two arts. I know very little about aesthetic philosophy, so I shall try, as far as possible, to speak from practical experience.

It is quite true that the artist, painter, writer or composer starts always with an experience that is a kind of discovery. He comes upon it with the sense of a discovery; in fact, it is truer to say that it comes upon *him* as a discovery. It surprises him. This is what is usually called an intuition or an inspiration. It carries with it always the feeling of directness. For instance, you go walking in the fields and all at once they strike you in quite a new aspect: you find it extraordinary that they should be like that. This is what happened to Monet as a young man. He suddenly saw the fields, not as solid flat objects covered with grass or useful crops and dotted with trees, but as colour in astonishing variety and subtlety of gradation. And this gave him a delightful and quite new pleasure. It was a most exciting discovery, especially as it was a discovery of something real. I mean, by that, something independent of Monet himself. That, of course, was half the pleasure. Monet had discovered a truth about the actual world.

This delight in discovery of something new in or about the world is a natural and primitive thing. All children have it. And it often continues until the age of twenty or twenty-five, *even* throughout life.

Children's pleasure in exploring the world, long before they can speak, is very obvious. They spend almost all their time at it. We don't speak of their intuition, but it is the same thing as the intuition of the artist. That is to say, it is direct knowledge of the world as it is, direct acquaintance with things, with characters, with appearance, and this is the primary knowledge of the artist and writer. This joy of discovery is his starting point.

Croce, probably the most interesting of the aesthetic philosophers, says that art is simply intuition. But he says, too, that intuition and expression are the same thing. His idea is that we can't know what we have intuited until we have named it, or given it a formal character, and this action is essentially the work of art.

But this is not at all the way it seems to an artist or a writer. To him, the intuition is quite a different thing from the work of art. For the essential thing about the work of art is that it is work, and very hard work too. To go back to the painter. He has had his intuition, he has made his discovery, he is eager to explore it, to reveal it, to fix it down. For, at least in a grown, an educated man, intuitions are highly evanescent. This is what Wordsworth meant when he wrote of their fading into the light of common day.

I said the joy of discovery often dies away after twenty years or so. And this is simply a truth of observation; we know it from our own experience. The magic object that started up before our eyes on a spring day in its own individual shape, is apt, in the same instant, to turn into simply another cherry tree, an ordinary specimen of a common class. We have seen it and named it pretty often already. But Housman, as poet, fixed his vision of the cherry tree before it had changed into just another tree in blossom.

Housman fixed it for himself and us, but not by an immediate act, indistinguishable from the intuition. He had to go to work and find words, images, rhyme, which embodied his feeling about the tree, which fixed down its meaning for him, so that he could have it again when he wanted it, and also give it to us. He made a work of art, but he made it by work.

So for the painter, when he has his new, his magic landscape in front of him; he has to fix it down. And at once he is up against enormous difficulties. He has only his paints and brushes, and a flat piece of canvas with which to convey a sensation, a feeling, about a three-dimensional world. He has somehow to translate an intuition from real objects into a formal and ideal arrangement of colours and shapes, which will still, mysteriously, fix and convey his sense of the unique quality, the magic of these objects in their own private existence. That is to say, he has a job that requires thought, skill, and a lot of experience.

As for the novelist, his case is even worse. He starts also with his intuition, his discovery; as when Conrad, in an Eastern port, saw a young officer come out from a trial, in which he had been found guilty of a cowardly desertion of his ship and its passengers after a collision. The young man had lost his honour and Conrad realised all at once what that meant to him, and he wrote *Lord Jim* to fix and communicate that discovery in its full force.

For that he had to invent characters, descriptions, a plot. All these details, as with the painter, had to enforce the impression, the feeling that he wanted to convey. The reader had to *feel*, at the end of the tale, 'That is important, that is true'. It's no good if he says, 'I suppose that is true, but I've heard it before'. In that case Conrad has failed, at least with that reader. For his object was to give the reader the same discovery, to make him feel what it meant to that young man to lose his honour, and how important honour is to men.

4

And to get this sharp and strong feeling, the reader must not be confused by side issues. All the scenes and characters, all the events in the book, must contribute to the total effect, the total meaning. The book must give the sense of an actual world with real characters. Otherwise they won't engage the reader's sympathy, his feelings will never be concerned at all.

But actual life is not like that, it doesn't have a total meaning, it is simply a wild confusion of events from which we have to select what we think significant for ourselves. Look at any morning paper. It makes no sense at all—it means nothing but chaos. We read only what we think important; that is to say, we provide our own sense to the news. We have to do so because otherwise it wouldn't be there. To do this, we have to have some standard of valuation, we have to know whether the political event is more important than a murder, or a divorce than the stock market, or the stock market than who won the Derby.

The writer, in short, has to find some meaning in life before he gives it to us in a book. And his subject-matter is much more confused than that of a painter. Of course, in this respect, everyone is in the same boat. Everyone, not only the writer, is presented with the same chaos, and is obliged to form his own idea of the world, of what matters and what doesn't matter. He has to do it, from earliest childhood, for his own safety. And if he gets it wrong, if his idea does not accord with reality, he will suffer for it.

5

A friend of mine, as a child, thought he could fly, and jumped off the roof. Luckily he came down in a flower-bed and only broke a leg.

This seems to contradict what I said just now about the chaos which stands before us every morning. For the boy who failed to fly did not suffer only from bad luck. He affronted a law of gravity, a permanent part of a reality objective to him. As we know very well, underneath the chaos of events, there are laws, or if you like consistencies, both of fact and feeling. What science calls matter, that is to say, certain fixed characteristics of being, presents us with a whole framework of reality which we defy at our peril. Wrong ideas about gravity or the wholesomeness of prussic acid are always fatal.

So, too, human nature and its social relations present certain constants. Asylums and gaols are full of people who have forgotten or ignored them. On the other hand, we can still comprehend and enjoy palaeolithic art and Homer. Homer's heroes had the same kind of nature as our own.

These human constants are also a part of reality objective to us, that is, a permanent character of the world as we know it. So we have a reality consisting of permanent and highly obstinate facts, and permanent and highly obstinate human nature. And human nature is always in conflict with material facts, although men are themselves most curious combinations of fact and feeling, and actually require the machinery of their organism to realise their emotions, their desires and ambitions. Though the ghost could not exist without the machine which is at once its material form, its servant, its limitation, its perfection and its traitor, it is always trying to get more power over it, to change it.

Men have in fact obtained more power over matter, but to change it is impossible. It may be said that all works of art, all ideas of life, all philosophies are 'As if', but I am suggesting that they can be checked with an objective reality. They might be called propositions for truth and their truth can be decided by their correspondence with the real. Man can't change the elemental characters. If you could, the world would probably vanish into nothing. But because of their very permanence, you can assemble them into new forms. You can build new houses with the bricks they used for the oldest Rome, because they are still bricks. For bricks that could stop being bricks at will would be no good to the architect. And a heart that stopped beating at its own will would be no good to the artist. The creative soul needs the machine, as the living world needs a fixed character, or it could not exist at all. It would be merely an idea. But by a paradox we have to accept, part of this fixed character is the free mind, the creative imagination, in everlasting conflict with facts, including its own machinery, its own tools.

II

ART AS MEANS

W E live in an everlasting battle, an ever-lasting creation which produces the endless revolution of politics and ideas that perplexes the morning paper. Of course, the turmoil of actual events is deeper than that. It is a true chaos; it includes an immense element of luck, of pure chance. For, although all events are determined, those that are ideas for action formed in some mind are partly self-determined and unpredictable. This brings uncertainty into every chain of causation where one link is the human will. What's more, so far as we are concerned as people, although all events belong to chains of causation, the chains are not synchronised. The individual going for a walk could not ascertain the chain of causes that sent a careful driver with a good car, an errand boy on a bicycle and a summer shower to combine in producing the skid that is going to kill him.

That is why a world of reality that possesses such definite forms both of fact and feeling, presents itself to us as chaos, a place full of nonsense, of injustice, of bad luck; and why children spend so much of their time asking questions. They are trying to build up, each for himself, some comprehensible idea by which to guide their conduct in such a terrifying confusion.

They find the task extremely difficult. Often they

get the wrong answers to their questions, and also they easily get the answers wrong. For words need interpretation and the interpretation depends very much, not only on the selection of the words, but the emphasis given to the words, on the quality of the words and on the tone of voice with which they are spoken. It is the selection, the emphasis, the tone, that gives the valuation. If a child is told, 'Don't eat too much cake', and 'Don't torture the cat', with the same mild emphasis, it will regard both actions with the same indulgence.

This selection, this tone, this emphasis is art. Almost all use of language is art, and particularly all communication between us, all communication that not only gives the facts, but also puts some valuation on the facts, is art. There is no other means by which the feeling about a fact can be conveyed.

This is because as children we are born with almost no instinct. We are almost entirely cut off from each other in mind, entirely independent in thought, and so we have to learn everything for ourselves. Hume pointed this out in his *Enquiry Concerning Human Understanding*, published in 1748, and no philosopher since has found an adequate answer to him. It is easy to see that if we were not so cut off from each other, if we were parts of a social commune, like ants or bees, we should not be free agents. Freedom, independence of mind, involves solitude in thought. We are not alone in feeling, in sympathy, but we are alone in mind, and so we are compelled, each of us, to form our own ideas of things, and if we want to convey these ideas and our feelings about them, we have to use art. Only art can convey both the fact and the feeling about the fact, for it works in the medium of common sympathies, common feeling, universal reaction to colour, sound, form. It is the bridge between souls, meaning by that not only men's minds but their character and feeling. And it carries almost all the traffic.

A punch on the nose is not art, but the words with which we attempt to justify it are certainly art, they are words with which we attempt to persuade, to describe and convey our emotion, to communicate an idea.

This may seem a large definition and overrides all the usual distinctions. I suppose most people think of art as pictures, symphonies, statues, poems, novels, what are often called the fine arts. This very distinction shows the feeling that art is something richer and larger than the art of the museums and libraries, and we find that in common discourse the word is used freely in the widest sense of any kind of activity from cooking to hairdressing. Journalism is definitely an art, and so is pleading in a law court, speaking in Parliament. I am choosing the widest definition, to begin with, because it seems to me the only true and significant one. My subject, as I said, is to be chiefly the arts I know, more especially the novel, but the novel is merely a special case of this universal art, and its special problems and function cannot be understood except in relation with the whole scene. So I am defining art as the means, and almost the only means, by which we can express ourselves in forms of meaning and communicate these meanings to others. It is the only means by which we can communicate both the fact and the feeling about the fact, which is, in our lives, always the most important thing. We can say that the whole impact of art is personal; it works in and by personality.

This takes us back to intuition, which is essentially the reaction of a person to the world outside. I said that the human child has very little instinct, that is, few innate patterns for conduct, but there is no doubt that it has, very early in life, a rich emotional equipment. Very small babies already have all the common feelings of affection, anger, jealousy. I think too that they have what one can call a primitive equipment of aesthetic response. Their response to different colours and different sounds is already particular. This is especially noticeable with sound. Certain sounds frighten them; cheerful rhythms please them. I think that even in very small children we find in embryo, but quite distinct, all those aesthetic feelings with which the grown and experienced lover of music listens to a symphony. Of course, such a listener brings to his enjoyment a great deal of knowledge about the technique of music, and a whole education in its appreciation, but the essential concentration is on sound, and the sounds, as organised, as a whole, carry a meaning. This meaning is for our emotions.

Yet it is meaning in the ordinary sense of the word, and descriptions in words of the emotional values of symphonic writing, so despised by music lovers, often do mean something significant. I agree that what they mean is not only the merest approximation to what the music means, but is also quite different in kind. That, of course, is why your music lover detests them. He is like a man who reads a translation of a classic known to him in his own tongue, tortured into some crude African dialect. He says, very naturally, 'This is a complete falsification'. But all the same, we do recognise that when the description speaks of tragic significance, it does approximate to a context in the music, and when it speaks of gaiety, that is something we also find in the notes and the rhythm. What I am suggesting, therefore, is that music deals with a complex set of emotional forms, of which the essential roots can be found in a small child, for they were inborn. This is not a question of innate ideas but innate feelings. And those of a small child may be said to belong to a world of universal forms. In mind and reason it is an individual, but in emotion, in fundamental sympathies, it belongs to a universal community.

Of course, the child also shows individual character from a very early age. But only, I suggest, a strictly independent character when it begins to reflect, to judge. Before that it simply reacts according to its emotional make-up. It is a piece of common reality of which the differentiation is simply that of one creature from another, with different potentiality and strength, different quality, as its seed belonged to a good or bad strain, but made of the same ingredients. As soon, however, as it begins to acquire knowledge, to reflect on it, to form ideas, it becomes a true individual soul. It can value the reality it knows, of emotions. It can form moral ideas, it can face a moral situation, which is always unique, and decide upon its response. It is not only independent, but obliged to be so, not only a moral being, but a solitary person in a dangerous world of vicissitude.

III

MIND AND FEELING

PERHAPS I should repeat here that this picture of things, as I give it, is not intended for an absolute truth; no one can know what that is. It is simply my own picture, as I see things. It is designed to lie close to my own experience. I haven't attempted to harmonise inconsistencies. For instance, I am here dealing with mind and feelings as separate entities, but we all know that they are never found apart and in ourselves belong to one whole. What's more, as we shall see, an education in ideas forms a character of feeling particular to that person.

When, therefore, I talk of reality and the individual

artist, I am using both words to describe the situation as it is known to us in actuality. For the individual, his feelings, his mind, his personality or character, are obviously part of some greater reality, they are made of it, they can't get outside it, even in imagination. It is impossible for us ever to think ourselves out of the universe, any more than a deep-sea fish can think itself out of the sea. But within this realm of being, we do recognise the distinction of the individual self from what is outside that self, and so I am writing of the individual as both separate from reality as creator and part of it as created.

What I'm suggesting here is that the child, in its feelings, in the subconscious, is not yet an individual. When, therefore, we say that intuition is discovery, revelation of the real, what I think really happens is that the emotional response of a child to form, colour and sound is in the first place automatic and immediate. They act upon the child's feelings as a certain note will set the strings of a violin ringing. The intuition is a subconscious recognition of the real, that takes place within a common personality.

This primary intuition of the child is not only of objects; it is also of feeling; possibly even of relations in feeling. Children of a year old will react at once to a mood in their mothers, or even to a mood between father and mother. All adults are aware of such an intuition as between husband and wife or friends; it is an emotional reaction in the subconscious. Thus we can say that all intuition takes place in the subconscious, and that it includes knowledge of feeling, sound, colour, rhythm, and so on, as well as of objects. Knowledge by intuition is like a flash between two electric poles. It is only after it has taken place that the mind asks, 'What has happened to me?'

In children, obviously, these electric flashes are going on all the time. Their minds are perpetually inquiring, 'What was that?' and I think it is significant that children's questions almost always concern the emotional impact of the outside world. They are not interested in objects as things except as they appear to sight, touch. They want to handle everything, to know what it feels like. Their first idea, for instance, of three-dimensional form is probably based on the feel of three-dimensional objects. They realise that things can have a fourth, hidden side because their fingers find it round the corner. Their knowledge of objects is, in the first place, by sensation.

I find some support in this view from the fact that an artist learns to disregard three-dimensional form if he chooses. He can see things as flat, or simply as coloured shapes, at will. That is to say, he returns deliberately to a world of knowledge as it exists before the idea and before the concept, a world consisting of pure forms for feeling.

This is obviously what happens in music, and that is why music has been described as the purest of the arts, why Schopenhauer said that all art strives towards the perfection of music. He meant that it has no mixture of factual representation; it does not depend for its effect on any allusion to fact. But Schopenhauer was himself an artist. He used language to convey his personal idea about the world, his personal feeling about the facts. All philosophy is art, and it can't escape from the predicament of the free independent mind compelled to use language, symbols, for the communication of its ideas. Modern philosophers have discovered what poets have known and complained of two thousand years ago: the inadequacy, the vagueness of words. They therefore doubt the possibility of conveying any truth by language and are attempting to invent mathematical signs to carry their philosophical ideas. Obviously the only ideas that can be conveyed by such signs will be mathematical ideas of quantity and dimension, relation and probability. If any attempt is made to convey quality and value, then the signs must become symbols capable of attaching to themselves the emotional supercharges which belong only to words as symbols.

IV

THE REALM OF PERSONALITY

IF any truth about quality, about the feeling as well as the fact, is to be conveyed from person to person, it can only be done within the realm of personality, of emotional and sensible forms, which is the world of art. The systematic philosopher, any philosopher, who attempts to convey any significant general idea about the world we know, the world we live in and suffer in, has like any other artist to select his facts to suit his idea. He has to devise a form to express and communicate his total meaning. And the form will dictate his valuation of details. This necessary bias appears very plainly in what philosophers say about art. Schopenhauer, for instance, exalts art because in contemplation of art man escapes from active desire, from willing, which for him is the supreme evil. He makes music the highest art because, as he argues, it represents pure will, pure desire, and so offers man by vicarious enjoyment the completest possible nirvana.

Plato calls it the imitation of objects because for him objects themselves were merely imitation, and as a moralistic dictator, hating and fearing the power of art, he wished to put art in the humblest possible place. Aristotle said it gave us the universal in the particular because in his scheme of the universe this relation of particular and universal was fundamental. So all philosophers, as you might expect, define art to suit their picture of things. Most of them express some truth. Plato was obviously thinking of the actual work of art, as an individual thing, Aristotle of some permanent element in actual appearance, like the beauty of colour and form which is the subject of all painters and sculptors.

Kant perceived one very true thing, that beauty does not need to have anything to do with morality or function. If we say 'What a pretty hat', we do not mean that it is a morally elevating hat or even that it will keep out the rain. On the other hand, Tolstoy and Ruskin declared that art is bad unless it has a moral purpose. And this has force too, because it disparages the theory of art for art's sake. It gives us the truth that it is only the most trivial arts that even pretend to serve a purely aesthetic end. Even hats are meant to attract attention. All great art has a meaning beyond itself.

Croce's statement, most interesting to a professional, that art is intuition, at once makes it a universal activity. For it is only by intuition that we have direct knowledge of the world. Croce gives art a necessary function in all life, in all history, private and social. For, according to Croce, when, by means of intuition, men know the world as it is, they set to work to act upon that knowledge. Contemplation of the actual is succeeded at once by reflection on its implications and possibilities, so men say, 'If this is what we have, we can and shall make something different'. We see the process going on all the time. For instance, in politics, governments are always telling us how they will change our world for the better, but, when they have brought in their Acts of Parliament, they are very surprised by the consequences, and begin to ask anxiously what exactly is happening, why this new world is behaving in such a strange and unexpected way; and a new crowd of observers sets to work to examine this new world, to see what it really is, and to write articles and books about it.

The philosophers select their facts to suit their systems, but all have some truth strictly limited by their idea. The work of art is an individual, unique thing. Even a newspaper article about absenteeism in the mines is unique. And it is art. It is a composition requiring selection, valuation. And again, the work of art always does have some reference to universal values: in this case, to human nature as it affects economics.

I'm not going to talk about beauty, because the word is ambiguous. Everything contemplated in its own essence is said to be beautiful, and to give pleasure. And Croce says it pleases us because it is also our expression and all expression is beauty. But a professional writer certainly distinguishes between beauty and ugliness, between what is repulsive and what is pleasing. For he uses the repulsive to get a definite effect. You may say that Flaubert's *Madame Bovary* is a work of complete beauty; but the death of Madame Bovary, by poison, is described in such a way as to disgust us—because Flaubert's fine taste knew that his tragedy required this ugly scene. So Croce's statement that all expression is beautiful is again the statement of an artist aiming at a beautiful neatness of construction. You can say, of course, that the beauty of Flaubert's work, taken as a whole, derives from a proportion in all the details. But the professional writer can reply that this perfect proportion requires the ugliness, the horror of Madame Bovary's death. And this is a real horror, founded in intuition. We know by it horror in the real, not only death but cruelty.

Flaubert has used ugliness to get his effect and the effect is moral. *Madame Bovary* is a morality, like all Flaubert's work. And, in fact, Tolstoy and Ruskin, in judging art by its moral effect, are doing no more than Flaubert intended. We do, in fact, make moral judgments about all art. We say, 'A pretty hat, but it proclaims the *cocotte*', that is to say, art has an effect in the actual world. Hence the perpetual war of the censors against the artist. Boccaccio's tales are agreed to be great art. But the Swindon magistrates wanted to burn them as dangerous to public morality. Genet's novels, ordered by the Birmingham libraries, were seized by the Post Office, which did not even bother to explain this action or to disclose why or by whom it was ordered. But the point here is not the evils and follies of censorship but the universal activity of art and the fear it inspires even in authority. The written and spoken arts are enormously powerful.

The influence of Rousseau, Voltaire, Diderot, on the French Revolution, or Turgenev and Dostoevsky and Tolstoy on the Russian, has been exaggerated, but it was extremely strong. And Marx's propaganda inspired the most powerful and widespread social revolution yet seen. His book became a bible to millions who carried out its message with the ardour of missionaries, the ardour that can be inspired only by dogma, by the assurance of truth and the promise of paradise.

And Marx is art. It is a picture of the economic world and economic history rendered harmonious and coherent by selection of those facts or apparent facts which fitted Marx's theory of the dialectic adapted from Hegel. It owes its power to its simplicity, and we do not find that simplicity in economics. They are as wildly confused as all the actual world, and therefore our feelings about economics are confused. We do not see any simple way to the millennium, we do not feel that paradise is round the corner if we take the trouble to turn it. But Marx, like Rousseau, made millions believe it, by the simplification of his idea and the rhetoric of his art. As for the great preachers, the orators, no one need doubt their power for good and evil. Wesley probably saved Britain a revolution of violence, Hitler wrecked Europe.

We can realise the power, day by day, of the press, the radio, the cinema. They are very obviously a great part of those creative forces which are changing the world all the time. Art, as creation in language, creates ideas, of which a very large proportion are, or become, ideas for action.

Of course, we have the best proof of the power of art in the fact that every dictator, every authority aspiring to complete control, from a church with its index to a local council that excludes the press, sets

21

up a censorship. And the more determined the
dictators, the more complete the censorship. Hitler
and Stalin attempted to control all the arts: painting,
sculpture and architecture, as well as the art of the
word.

V

WHAT MEN LIVE BY

THE reason is that art expresses and communicates feelings and desires, and that men live
by their feelings and desires. What they seek
in life from the very beginning is to satisfy various
appetites and emotional needs. For that they require
an idea of the world in which they have to succeed,
from which they have to obtain satisfaction. They
want a guide to life as navigators want a map, so that
they shan't run on destruction before they find port.
Guides to life, however, even before they come to
interpretation by the individual, differ so much that
the young are apt to be bewildered. A good many
give up all hope of any clear and reliable guide very
early indeed, even in their teens. But the desire
remains and it is very urgent. That is why any new
creed presenting a complete guide is so sure of
popularity among students, why Marxism, Fabian-
ism, Nazism, spiritualism, any new 'ism' which
offers a complete picture, even a depressing picture,
like Spenglerism or behaviourism, has such immense appeal to anyone under thirty. They set free;

22

they give a coherent set of values, in which emotions formerly in conflict, and therefore frustrated, can suddenly find complete satisfaction. Everyone has noticed the self-confidence of the Marxist convert. The neurotic and frustrated muddle-head of a month ago, uncertain and bewildered in every contact, in every relation, has become completely sure of himself and full of eagerness to realise this world that he has now found, to realise himself, to enjoy himself in that world. That is why he is also indifferent to facts or argument. He does not accept any fact that would injure his new faith, in which alone he finds his way in life.

This desire for the guide, the clear picture which sets free, is so urgent that almost any dogmatic statement, so long as it is simple and clear, will be accepted. Tolstoy's anarchism carried such weight because it was the simplest of all. Tolstoy said in effect, do nothing, leave it all to God, who is found in our own human nature. This fiction carried a unique emotional appeal. It offered a golden age of peace and love and happiness, which was to be attained at once, much sooner than the Marxian. Tolstoy did not promise merely that the State would wither when evil had vanished from the world and all men were always good; he said that if the State were at once abolished, all men would be good, and universal happiness would begin.

In fact, men live so entirely by feeling that reason has extremely small power over even our most intelligent, our geniuses like Marx and Tolstoy. If you don't believe this, you only have to look at the papers, at day-to-day politics. We see there how little reason, how little even common prudence, can restrain whole peoples, or their leaders, from actions which amount to suicide when they are offered a chance of gratifying such entirely egotistic passions as greed, hatred, revenge, pride, wounded self-esteem or, most powerful, most persistent and most reckless of all, an inferiority complex. This is not to say that they are completely selfish. On the contrary, passions are often regardless of self; a man will cheerfully die for such an ideal and abstract notion as a religious faith, a country which does not even exist except as a name, or merely for duty and honour, the good name of his regiment or family.

Thus the most important part of man's existence, that part where he most truly lives and is aware of living, lies entirely within the domain of personal feeling. Reason is used only to satisfy feeling, to build up a world in which feelings can be gratified, ambition realised; and, as we see in history, even then it has very little power in conflict with any strong emotion, any powerful symbol like a flag, the mere name of a country, even one invented last week, or words like 'freedom'.

The new inventions, radio and television, have enormously increased this turmoil, because they have increased the power of the word, of rhetoric, of the demagogue. And education, which is demanded

24

by all peoples and provided by all governments, itself makes millions more restless, more dissatisfied, more ready to listen to the demagogues. Never before in history has the word, in speech and book, the picture on the cinema or on television, the dogma in some national or commercial slogan, had such power. And they have produced such a confusion of ideologies and militant nationalisms that a great many people despair of civilisation as it is. They expect the world to tumble once more into a thousand years of barbarism.

So we have new demands for censorship all over the world, and new censorships imposed by governments. Their excuse is always the same, that artists and writers distort the truth. But censorship in history always has the same result; sooner or later it produces corruption, frustration and cynicism in whole peoples. It fosters the black-market of rumour and suspicion and undermines the State with secret hatred of all authority and, worse, contempt for its fears, a keen perception of its weakness.

A people treated like irresponsible morons will behave like irresponsible savages—the Teddy boy adolescent toting a spring-knife to swagger away his own miserable sense of ignorance and self-contempt is only the Teddy boy nation writ small.

To suppress the freedom of the arts is not only to cut off knowledge of the actual movements of human feeling but also, and more disastrously, contact with the realities of life. For those contacts can be renewed only by the continually new intuition of the artist.

VI

ART AND TRUTH

ART claims to give us truth. According to Croce, in fact, the primary work of art, the expression, must be true, because it is indistinguishable from intuition. This is essential to Croce's aesthetic philosophy. He says that if we deny it his system becomes impossible, for at once we place a great gap between reality and our knowledge of it, an unbridgeable gap. To put it in his own words, we 'divide the seamless robe of the world'.

As I say, Croce's system is probably the most harmonious, the most beautiful of any in its graceful and economical forms. But it is art. And to obtain those harmonies Croce has ignored certain matters of experience, and most notable, the gap between intuition and expression. Every professional artist knows this gap. It is for him a fundamental problem. Tolstoy tells us in his diary how he sat for a long time trying to express his feeling; but he could not find the right words. What is interesting to us is that Tolstoy's feeling—the intuition—remained to be examined, to be compared with the various expressions which were rejected in turn because they failed to be accurate.

What the intuition consisted of here was an impression on the memory, an impression of feeling. It was emotion directly intuited and recorded. Such intuitions are often recorded without our being aware of them. We are asked, 'Did you meet So-and-so? What did you think of him?' And remembering So-and-so, we explore our minds, that is to say, some record in the subconscious, to find out what we did think of him. And we are conscious of this effort of exploration; like Tolstoy we look for words to express our feeling, our reaction, and don't find them at once. Tolstoy tells us that he found the task so exasperating he wanted to get up and walk away. There is no short cut across this gap.

The passage from intuition to reflection, from knowledge of the real to expression of that knowledge in viable form is always precarious and difficult. It is, in short, a kind of translation, not from one language into another, but from one state of existence into another, from the receptive into the creative, from the purely sensuous impression into the purely reflective and critical act.

This gap, of course, is simply another representative of the mind-body gap, which all idealist philosophers and mechanists are so eager to get rid of: the first by abolishing the body and the second by abolishing the mind. Unfortunately, though they can contrive this abolition easily enough in words, it remains very definite to our experience. All of us are aware every day of the conflict between our will and bodily machine; no amount of willing, no amount of thinking can compel the body to be completely subservient. On the other hand, we are equally aware of their interdependence; mind needs body to exist and body needs mind for any purposeful activity; that is to say, this gap of which we are so acutely aware occurs within a unity. If we could imagine a motor-car complaining of the gap in its spark-plugs, we should hasten to explain to it that the gap, though certainly existing, is not only an essential part of its construction as a complete unity, but that without this gap it could not work.

In fact, it would be easy to argue that without the gap between body and mind the individual would not exist; he would be merely a part of universal nature, controlled completely by instinct, with all the limitations of creatures whose lives are so controlled. It is the independent reason of man in which his individuality, his freedom, resides. The gap is as necessary to him as the division between his feet and the ground, which enables him, unlike a vegetable, to move about the world by his own volition.

This suggestion itself is merely an attempt in words to suggest an explanation of something which lies beneath and beyond language and its logical systems, and in this essay I am trying to deal with a situation as known to experience; the dilemma of the free individual soul, separated by the very nature of his individuality from the real of which he is nevertheless a part.

It will be seen that this description in words itself falsifies the problem by the mere analysis of an essential unity into the individual on one side and reality on the other; a false dichotomy is introduced and what is highly flexible in practice is given the appearance of rigid and permanent separation. As we should see, the gap itself between body and mind, even to our experience, is not fixed; it varies from individual to individual and continually shifts its place. The gap is not between the individual and the outer world; it is in the man, between his individual mind seeking to know a truth, and the universal consistencies of nature human and material as recorded by his sensibility. That sensibility in a grown man is, of course, individual and particular. His primitive emotions have been given ideal form by his experience and education. But they are still primitive in essence. The child's love for those who tend and feed it has become the mature affection full of judgment and particular appreciation. But it is still love, still within the universal of feeling and objective to the individual mind. That is to say, the educated man is still, in his primitive emotional make-up, part of the universal real. His difference is only ideal and formal, just as a house, however distinctive in itself, is still part of material nature.

In the larger sense, of course, that individual mind is also part of the universal real. All humanity is born with it. And we know it ourselves by experience.

Total reality is given to us in this divided form. Croce's 'seamless world' presents itself to us as deeply seamed; the individual mind appears to itself as cut off from the general real except in so far as it can intuit that real. For the artist his intuition always comes to him as from a world of permanent and objective forms. What Tolstoy was looking for was not his own idea of things, but the exact impression they had made on him.

No doubt that intuition contained some elements of choice. It moved Tolstoy in a certain way because he was Tolstoy—with his special sensibility. For no one after the first few months of life retains the primitive emotions as pure general feeling. The moment a child begins to think and record its reflections, judgments begin to attach themselves to its emotions. Its individual mind, so to speak, begins to soak into its emotional make-up. This, in fact, is the process often described as forming a character. But to this character compounded of educated and ideal emotion and a presiding mind, the intuition comes always as a revelation. This is how it appears to the man. It is the very mark and sign of intuition that it does so appear, from outside. It stands over against him, like Housman's cherry tree, a piece of the real whose whole force is in its objectivity and universal truth. And he, as subject, has to use his brains to translate the effect of this real into a symbolic form which gives the same effect to another person.

His problem is to transmit a purely emotional meaning by the same kind of effort that is used to solve a chess problem. In this effort, therefore, there is a direct conflict. A cold thought has to deal with a warm feeling. I said that intuitions are evanescent. Wordsworth's intuitions die not only for the man, they fade very quickly for the child. But conceptual thought cannot only destroy them, it can bar them out.

This is an old tale. The child genius goes to school and becomes a dull man. What we have to ask is why this conflict occurs; if it is inevitable, how anything of the real can pass the gap between the intuition and the expression, the work of art; and, in short, whether art is not, as dictators like to believe, purely subjective and fantastic, the dangerous amusement of a lot of egotistic parasites.

VII

THE REALM OF INTUITION

INTUITION, the recognition of the objective real in its own quality, is, of course, an essential function. The smallest children must have power to know. And they explore the world of things and events, of characters, with intense curiosity and concentration.

I remember one of my children, as a baby of about fourteen months, sitting in its pram watching a newspaper on the grass close by. There was a breeze along the ground and the newspaper was moving. Sometimes the top page swelled up and fluttered; sometimes two or three pages were moved and seemed to struggle together; sometimes the whole paper rose up on one side and flapped awkwardly for

31

a few feet before tumbling down again. The child did not know that this object was a newspaper moved by the wind. It was watching with intense absorbed curiosity a creature entirely new to its experience, and through the child's eyes I had a pure intuition of the newspaper as object, as an individual thing at a specific moment.

The same child, at six, painted a little masterpiece of a tiger in a wood. The wood was practically solid tree trunk—the only indication of branches or leaves was a few minute strokes of brown and spots of green at the extreme top. In fact, a wood intensely seen by a child's eye in its woodiness, and expressed with the highest degree of original force.

A great deal, of course, of that spiritual and perpetual joy that children bring to us is just this power of seeing the world as a new thing, as pure intuition, and so renewing for us the freshness of all life. But they always lose this power of original expression as soon as they begin their education. A small girl of seven once asked me if I would like a drawing. I said yes. She asked. 'What shall I draw?'

'Anything you like.'

'Shall I draw you a swan?'

'Yes, a swan'; and the child sat down and drew for half an hour. I'd forgotten about the swan until she produced the most original swan I'd ever seen. It was a swimming swan, that is, a creature designed simply to swim. Its feet were enormous and very carefully finished, obviously from life. The whole structure of the feet was shown in heavy black lines. The child was used to seeing swans on a canal at the end of her garden and had taken particular notice of their feet. Below the water the swan was all power. But for body she gave it the faintest, lightest outline, neck and wings included in one round line shaped rather like a cloud—a perfect expression of the cloud-like movement of the swan on the surface.

I was admiring this swan when an older child in the room, aged thirteen, looked at the drawing and said contemptuously 'That's not a bit like a swan. I'll draw you a swan,' and produced at once a Christmas-card swan, of the commonest type.

Yet the second child had all the qualities of the first, intelligence, sensibility. A few years before she had had the ability to see for herself, to receive the unique personal impression. She had lost it by the education which emphasises the fact, measurements, analysis, the concept. Education is, and must be, almost entirely conceptual. And the concept is always the enemy of the intuition. It is said that when you give a child the name of a bird, it loses the bird. It never *sees* the bird again but only a sparrow, a thrush, a swan, and there is a good deal of truth in this. We all know people for whom all nature and art consists of concepts, whose life, therefore, is entirely bound up with objects known only under labels and never seen in their own quality.

This ruin of aesthetic intuition by conceptual education has been the theme of teachers for at least fifty years past, and has produced the theory that children should not be taught anything about the arts. They should be assisted, if necessary, only in handling materials. But this is futile. For children want to learn, they are greedy to know, they triumph over each other in knowledge. If you do not teach them they will learn from each other, and probably learn wrong. The attempt to preserve the intuition of the child, in any art, is therefore waste of time. It can be disastrous if it results only in the production of an imitative childishness, a self-conscious *naïveté* which is more stultifying than any mere conventionalism.

Yet Picasso has said, 'Give me the mind of a child,' and Picasso himself has shown more freshness of intuition and invention, more fertile originality, than any artist in centuries. All the same, Picasso is a product of the schools, he is highly accomplished in technique. He has given immense thought to the problem of artistic expression. And as a young artist he showed all the conventionality of the art student just graduated from years of conceptual teaching in the drawing class. His blue period is the cliché of a student mind attempting originality merely by style and achieving therefore not only the false but the conventional. For nothing is more easy than the novel style invented only to be different.

That is to say, Picasso has passed from the age of true childish inspiration, through years of conceptual and technical training, back to the original vision which is not childish, but has all the originality of the child's eye, combined with the far greater depth and richness of a man's experience.

It may be said—it is sometimes believed—that Picasso's originality is merely a calculated scorn of convention, a deliberate resolution to shock, by what is called wilful distortion. That is to say, that it is not founded on intuition at all, but on a conceptual plan. This would be believed only by those without power to appreciate any original art at all. And it can be tested by anyone who should choose to set out, deliberately, to produce an effect of originality simply by a conceptual difference.

VIII

ORIGINALITY

PICASSO is not extraordinary, except in his power and fertility. His career has been the normal one of every artist. All show, as students, a conventional and conceptual manner of expression. All lose what originality they had, and, if they attempt originality, produce sophisticated imitations of their own first efforts, or of some reigning master. It is only later, set free from the schools, that they may show once more real individual quality. As we know, most of them don't. Probably 90 per cent of all students never attain any original expressive power. But those who do fill up the total

35

category of great and original artists. As far as I can see, there is no way out of this dilemma.

But the academic training is always under suspicion and lately we have had a new angle of attack. Here is an extract from a letter to *The Times* of June 1956: 'The representation of natural appearances is no longer an indispensable or even a characteristic function of the art of painting. The criterion of truth to nature, unless interpreted in some esoteric sense, has ceased to be of critical importance. The artist is now at liberty to distort appearances as inspiration or folly may suggest.' And lower down: 'It has been officially recognised that the elaborate course of instruction formerly provided for the student of fine art is now out of date.' And the writer wants to abolish examinations in technique and declares the Royal College superfluous.

This has a new and contemporary look because the writer bases his argument on the statement that a painter need no longer imitate nature. He says that if anyone wants to paint in 'naturalistic style' he can work from photographs. This last remark is so silly that the writer, I suspect, is either a disgruntled Academician who hates abstract art and is crying out like the typical dictator, in defeat, 'If I can't have what I want, I'll burn the world,' or a philistine who knows nothing whatever of the plastic arts. For, without knowledge of anatomy, it is even more difficult to draw from the photograph than the living model. In both cases it is quite impossible to draw well. It is impossible to make that emphasis which gives meaning and quality to a drawing, an emphasis which often distorts. You can see it in Rodin as well as Henry Moore.

But if, as I suspect, the anonymous writer of this letter knows all this very well, if he is merely making a violent protest against abstract art, his case is one for sympathy. He is one of those unhappy people who see their taste go out of fashion. He is at one with the critics who said that Walt Whitman was not a poet, and that Pre-Raphaelite art showed the lowest depths of what is mean, odious, repulsive and revolting—this in reference to Millais' carpenter's shop. He is objecting to a change in the form and significance of the symbol, a revolution which is one of the fundamental conditions and problems of all creative art. And we are going to consider that special problem below (Section 16, p. 71).

But, whatever his motive, he will receive enthusiastic support. In fact, he has received it. For there are always plenty of honest and energetic people who regard all systematic education as corruption of the young and innocent, that it belongs to the dark ages of the world when tyrants laid down the law in every department of life. Any such attack on any teaching institution is immensely popular; it promises the student glory without work, it suggests that there is no real difference between the educated and the uneducated man. Or, rather, that the latter is the superior. Tolstoy thought or tried to think the Russian peasant the wisest man in the world. It appeals very strongly to that deep and strange passion which we find in every generation for what is called the return to nature. Every day we hear abuse of civilisation and all its culture by the simple-lifer who wants to live like Thoreau and put off the corruption of the world. But Thoreau was a highly educated man. The real simple-lifer, the aboriginal, leads a very hard life by rules and tabus far more oppressive than those of any citizen of London or New York. It is the man of culture, the scholar, who really simplifies his life. It is only very wise and learned men who have the freedom of a quiet mind, and they do not achieve it by running away from civilisation, and denouncing its culture and its scholarship.

IX

EDUCATION

WITHOUT education, it is not possible for a man even to appreciate any art. For education does not give only knowledge, but taste; it qualifies the feelings as well as the judgment. It creates the sensibility which is a compound of feeling and judgment—the depths of a man's sensibility, the sureness of his judgment, will be in proportion with the thoroughness of his education. And the education must, in the first place, be factual. I am speaking from experience. When I went to an art school I was set to learn anatomy, and to model anatomical forms: hands, feet, eyes, ears, mouths. The latter were always made about four times life-size, and from ideal originals. This was to show all the modelling which is almost imperceptible in life. In the mouth, especially, there are subtle forms about the corners of the lips, subtle changes in the curve of lips, subtle contrasts between upper and lower lips, which are not even perceived by an observer who does not know how and where to look for them. So, too, the setting of the eye, different in every person, the bulge of the cornea on the eye-ball, according to the direction of the gaze, cannot be seized by the most acute observer without some knowledge of anatomy. If he does notice a detail, he doesn't know what it means, whether it is an idiosyncracy in the model, a deformity, or a shape common to all eyes in that special position. And his drawing will show his ignorance, his indecision. What's more, he will not be able even to see the fine points in drawing. He will be blind to them as a man who never learnt grammar and syntax is blind to the fine points of style.

And there is no such thing as imitation in art. All art involves translation. The most careful school drawing from the model is not the model—it is a representation in pencil or charcoal on the flat, and every touch requires thought and skill, knowledge of materials and their limitations, and an idea of what general effect is intended. We distinguish very easily between the distortions of Michelangelo, El Greco and Picasso. Each is aiming at a different ideal effect. But in each case what is beautiful in the very distortion is the treatment of the anatomical forms, the reference to the real. They are not arbitrary quirks of fancy, mere arabesques without meaning in themselves, but allusions, symbols carrying all the more implications in that they are both scholarly and freely imaginative. Picasso's etchings are full of wit, but it is the wit of a scholar. Henry Moore's sculpture relies on the same quality, it refers everywhere to the forms of the real, it is full of scholarship.

But, we are told, what's true for the plastic artist is not true for the writer. It is obvious that painters, sculptors, composers, architects must have an elaborate education. And this education in technique and in styles is blamed for turning out men who have no ideas beyond the reproduction of Palladian façades or pastiches of Stravinsky.

This is a hazard, obviously, that composers and architects must run. Their technical equipment cannot be picked up by the way, it requires long and specialised study. But many great novelists have had, apparently, very little formal teaching. Dostoevsky and Dickens are described in common speech as self-educated. Tolstoy declares himself to be so, for though he had tutors at home, he left the university after a single year.

Actually every child gets a long and highly conceptual education at home, in ideas, in conduct. And every schoolboy learns to handle words and to write. That is why a person who is described as illiterate can often speak and write with such force, where his drawings or compositions would be quite worthless. Everyone except an actual idiot acquires a certain amount of literary education—ideas, however confused, to express, and the elementary technical power to express them.

And we notice that the most powerful influence in both Tolstoy's and Dostoevsky's mature work is precisely the formal and dogmatic religious training of their childhood. It is true that, like James Joyce, they reacted against it in their different ways. But they never escaped from it. Tolstoy repudiated the Church only to fall back into the primitive Christian anarchism of the desert monk; Dostoevsky said, 'If Christ was on one side and truth on the other, I should follow Christ'. In fact he was continually tempted to fly into the truth. In that great scene of *The Brothers Karamazov* where Ivan argues against his brother Alyosha's faith, the chapter called 'Pro and Contra', it was Ivan who produced the most crushing arguments. They were so strong that Dostoevsky himself was terrified. He feared the Government censors. He wrote to all his religious and orthodox friends to tell them that in the very next instalment he would bring in his priest, the saintly father Zossima, to answer Ivan. He spent weeks on those fifty pages which were to give the refutation. And, after all his work, he failed most dismally.

But notice that, though Dostoevsky is contradictory, he is never confused. He gives a sharp edge to all the arguments, he states every position with clarity and force. He shows that power of logical grasp which comes only from a dogmatic education. For dogma is the anatomy of thought. As scientists tell you, even a bad doctrine is better than none at all. You can test it, differ from it, your mind has something to bite on. You need the rock to plan the lighthouse.

'Pro and Contra' is a monument to the integrity of the artist who loved truth a great deal better than he knew. And also it shows us how deep and strong were the effects of Dostoevsky's religious education as a child.

Where Dickens picked up his effective ideas we don't know. But they were not only contradictory but confused. He relied on sentiment to inform his judgment, and sentiment is blind. Sometimes he writes like an anarchist, who hates all authority as the root of evil, sometimes like a reformer who denounces the weakness of government. The anarchist and the fascist or communist are, of course, brothers under the skin. Both say, 'I know what's right and if anyone contradicts me he's a wicked man and ought to be destroyed'.

Dickens' ambiguities are common to every sentimentalist who creates a dream-world for himself. He was essentially a poet, his books are like ballads, and his greatness is in his power to transport us into a region of fantasy almost purely emotive. He makes us laugh and even cry, makes us drunk with words, but he never makes us think. Of all the great masters he has the least appeal to reason. Compared with Jane Austen, George Eliot, Thackeray, the great Russians who admired him so much, he is boneless. And this is what we might expect. For, whatever his education, it was not systematic.

To put this problem of the writer's education in short form we can suggest that if Dickens had had a more solid education, he could have been the greatest of all novelists, or equally, he might never have written at all.

This, of course, is to reflect that the genius, like everyone else in the world, has to reckon with luck. Who can say whether that blacking factory in which Dickens worked as a boy and suffered such humiliation did harm or good to his creative imagination, or how much we owe to the fact that Dostoevsky's father was tortured to death by his serfs, or that he himself was sentenced to be shot, and pardoned only at the place of execution? What is due in Tolstoy to the insensate arrogance of the provincial noble? Was James Joyce's obsessive ambition the product of his humiliation as the son of a feckless father, or of the rigid scholastic training which formed so powerful and self-confident a will to mastery?

43

X

VALUE AND MEANING

THE growth of every soul is mysterious and full of chances. It is the dream of every Utopian to throw luck out of the world—the luck of birth, of brains, of beauty, of fate—to make all destinies equal. That is a dream that can't be realised. The world is inescapably shot through with luck, because it is also shot through with freedom. It is in the field given over to luck, the field of the unconditioned, that the free soul operates, and one man's art is another's luck, one teacher's prejudice is the making or the ruin of a poet.

Luck remains and children will always have different abilities, different kinds of home, different fates, in experience. But it is still the duty of government and parents to battle with luck, to try to give the equal chance. And the front of that battle is education. The education of the writer is necessarily the education offered to other children, and what I am arguing is that it can't be too good, too definite. You can't preserve his youthful intuition. The child poet and writer, in my own experience, loses his powers even more quickly than the child painter. For he starts his education in the arts of the word, he is getting ideas about life, while the other is still being allowed to amuse himself with a colour-box.

No one, in short, escapes a conceptual and technical education in the use of words and ideas, and the only question is, how good should it be. I'm saying that it should be as good as possible. For the chance of destroying an original genius by too much scholarship, too rigid a conceptual drill, is much less than that of leaving him, when at last he is ready to do mature work, with a muddled mind' and a feeble grasp of elementary technique.

The most sensible critic of the artistic education agrees to the absolute necessity of factual and conceptual knowledge and a dogmatic framework to give these facts value and meaning. But he says the trouble is not there but in the bias of the teachers who convey their own prejudices, who try to form their pupils' tastes, to bring them to be little copies of their teachers. This, he says, is the real disaster in academic education, not only for artists, but musicians, writers, architects. The old men who have a grip on all the schools, on all the universities, hate the original mind. They can't understand it and, as pedants, they hate what they can't understand. Why not then get rid of this bias and find teachers without it? Let them teach without bias. Let them teach the facts, suggest a meaning for the facts, offer a theory to explain them, but not as an irrefutable dogma. For instance, let them say of poetry, 'This is Wordsworth's theory about good writing, but it was not Pope's. Take your choice.' Or of history, 'This is how Marx explains the march of events, and this is the Cambridge history. Here are the arguments, make up your own mind.'

There is a lot of truth and sense in this argument. For most teaching, especially in the arts, has a good deal of bias. The fact that students catch their tastes as well as their ideas from their teachers, that the pupils of an art school copy the style of some dominant master, is a commonplace. And there is no doubt it is a pretty common cause why some at least of them never form an original idea or style. But can your teacher hide his bias? If he does, will he be any good as a teacher? Is not the good teacher precisely a man of strong convictions who can put them over?

When I was at school, I wrote certain essays for which I was given prizes. And the two masters who chiefly encouraged me were both remarkable men. One had real genius, Grey. He taught the upper fourth. It consisted of lively young boys of fourteen or so, on their way to the fifth, and enormous blockheads of seventeen, tottering on the edge of superannuation, but mostly quite resigned to it. They weren't by any means all fools. A lot of them, for one reason or another, had simply decided to fight against education of any kind. Their chief glory was to be lowbrows. Yet Grey made some of them enjoy Shakespeare so much that they read the plays for themselves—one, I know, carried a Temple Shakespeare in his pocket for the rest of his life, and so far became not only an educated man but a very interesting person. Grey did this chiefly by reading the plays aloud. He would sit on his desk and act them for us. I had only one term with him, but he gave me an unforgettable and important experience.

The other remarkable man was Sydney Irwin, who opened his library to me. Irwin was a precise and careful scholar who did, I believe, a good deal of reviewing for *The Times* of that date. And he encouraged me to write. Unluckily, he was anxious not to impress his own judgments, he tried as far as possible to leave me to express my own ideas in my own way. The result was that I did not learn to use language with precision, and years later had to struggle with problems that I should have had solved for me at school. I found these prize essays some years ago, and they had the faults no schoolboy should be allowed to commit, and what's more, their ideas were extremely conventional.

For I was perfectly aware that I had gone to school to learn, and Irwin, like Grey, had his preferences, his own formed taste. The only difference between them as teachers was that Grey made no secret of preferences, and Irwin sought to hide them. He succeeded too well. So, in my essays, I imitated anthology pieces.

Boys want an education as children seek knowledge. They want to know how and what to think, and it is not even certain whether, in the ages between ten and sixteen or later, they have any real creative energy in their imagination. I suspect it is largely taken up with growing, as their minds are taken up with gathering facts and technique.

Irwin, with all the good will in the world, gave me only encouragement. It was perhaps more valuable than I supposed. But I could have had the knowledge too, and I couldn't get that anywhere else. How could I know that I'd missed it? It is the tragedy of the world that no one knows what he doesn't know—and the less a man knows, the more sure he is that he knows everything.

I knew Grey only for a month or two, but he was an enthusiast, a man of the strongest literary prejudice. For him, Shakespeare was the only master that mattered. Often in his zest while reading, he obviously forgot all about us in the form. Grey gave me something of the profoundest value. As I say, he transformed lives, he saved some pretty hopeless lives. He had genius, and he had enthusiasm. But you don't have enthusiasm without bias.

In the same way, the man who taught me most about drawing in the art school was the one with strong prejudices. He liked only one kind of drawing, the classical. He would have loathed Picasso if he had ever heard of him. He would glance at my drawing of a model and say, 'You don't know what you're doing, do you? Here, what's that *mean*?' Pointing, say, at a shadow on the back. I would say, 'It's on the model', and he would answer fiercely, 'But what is it—muscle or dirt? What's it *mean*?'

This was his cry all the time: 'What's it mean?' He would point at a knee and say, 'Look at that piece of boiled macaroni. What's that line mean there? Which leg is she standing on?'

'The left.'

'Then why don't you show the tension in the hamstrings?'

'It's in shadow.'

'What's that matter? You're not trying to be a camera. You're trying to tell us something,' and he'd take my pencil and do what I hated, slash in a line on top of my drawing. 'Now at least she can stand up on her own legs.'

I don't think this man had much enthusiasm for drawing. But he had a set of principles and he was perfectly sure they were right. He taught me exactly what I needed to know about drawing, the fundamental rules, the logic, the syntax. Teaching, in short, like everything else that conveys a meaning in words, is an art, and you can't be a good artist unless you believe you are giving a truth. The most effective teacher will always be biased, for the chief force in teaching is confidence and enthusiasm. To give merely information is to write on the sand. For it is his function to form a character of feeling about ideas and to do that he has to have pretty strong feelings himself, as well as clear ideas.

All the great painters of the past—Giotto, Rembrandt, Rubens, Watteau, Gainsborough, Reynolds —began as apprentices in a studio where they ground the colours and learnt by rote, like young plumbers. 'This is the right way to do the job, and there isn't any other.' They were expected to put in a background so like the master's that it would pass for his own work.

This, too, is the usual and universal education given to children in the nursery by parents of any strong and definite view, political or religious. The significant thing about Dostoevsky and Tolstoy, James Joyce and many more, is the permanent cast given to their minds and feelings by early religious training. Their genius was in their use of that training to make new and original works of art.

XI

NATIVE GENIUS

IT is dogmatic training which is most likely to destroy the native intuition of the child, but I'm not certain that this is much of a misfortune.

In the first place, I doubt if young genius, if the child's intuition, is worth preserving. Child art is charming, and original, but it is very small art. It is at best simply a cry of exhilaration, a nursery lyric. Much of the pleasure we take in it is a highly sophisticated enjoyment of innocence. We delight in the drawing of a scene, not because it is really telling us anything new or interesting about an actual scene, but because it is an unconscious parody of the academies.

Child art can never be great art. It cannot give any large meaning to the world, any new revelation of the truth, because the child mind cannot have enough knowledge and experience of the world to form any true comprehensive ideas about it. So if we are to have any great painters, any great writers, there has to be education, and that education will have to be largely conceptual, and so destructive of the original intuitive power.

But this destruction goes deep. For, as we said, education forms character. It gives ideal form and direction to the emotions. When Grey taught those blockheads to enjoy Shakespeare he changed the nature of their feelings about poetry, at least, about Shakespeare's poetry. By making them share his sympathetic reactions, he changed them into different persons.

As consolation for this enormous destruction of native genius we are assured that it doesn't last, it doesn't really matter, that real genius always comes through. And we hear of Keats, Shelley, Cézanne, Lawrence, all those who have come through in spite of every discouragement. But I don't believe a word of it. I've lived long enough to see a lot of genius that never got a chance. I believe, in fact, that genius, meaning by that an original creative power, is both much more common than we suppose and much more fragile. It is certainly more fragile than talent. For talent belongs to the capable and intelligent who understand their own powers and know how to manage them. Genius is sensitive and impression-able. The brilliant child with its intuitive play becomes the highly-strung boy whose feelings are a great deal too quick and confused for his brain. Flaubert remarked once that child prodigies never come to anything because they never learn to ride their fevers. This is not quite true, but it is true that brilliant children of strong feeling are often overwhelmed by the confusion of the world before they have time to get a clue to its meaning for them or to control their own reactions.

This is not the only trap for genius. Its road is full of holes. It can be too modest and accept the view of some early critic that it is no good. I would bet that many a fine career has been cut off in the judgment of some admired friend. Or your young artist marries young and, being a decent fellow, takes money-making jobs to keep his wife and children from starving. Or he is a Van Gogh who never went to Paris to discover the new technique of Impressionism, so exactly fitted to express his intuition; a Nelson without a fleet or a Liszt born before the piano.

A genius needs luck to come through at all and part of his luck, it seems, may be that kind of education which is also most dangerous to him—for we see that it is just the most intensive and dogmatic training that can produce the most towering genius, such as Dante, Goethe, Milton, Dostoevsky, Tolstoy, Joyce; and also that it is most potent to frustrate the original mind. For it may turn that mind in another direction towards the critical art of the scholar.

The scholar, of course, is also a creative artist, but

he creates his idea, his world, from what he has learned; he builds his career, his life upon it, or rather within it. He is a creator, but his subject matter is the work of art, the thing made. He loves and serves the beauty that exists. The original artist either accepts that beauty, that formal construction of feeling and idea, as matter of course, and takes off from it into new invention, or he reacts violently against it. Jane Austen took the Anglican world as given to her, loved it, and enlarged upon it. Its ideals, so firmly grasped and strongly accepted, set her free. Her beautiful clarity, her mastery, is that of one who has no moral doubts, whose judgment is always confident. Her command of form is due to her command of a moral idea—her greatness to the fact that her moral idea was true within its context.

XII

DEATH OF OLD SYMBOLS

JANE AUSTEN belongs to the school of great art which affirms and develops an existing school. Fielding and Richardson were her masters, but she refined upon them, with more subtlety than Fielding, more economy than Richardson; like those architects who, generation after generation, so brilliantly developed the Romanesque through all the Gothic forms because they were soaked in the Gothic idea, and could not imagine any other. Their originality was founded on an intense pleasure in the Gothic world, and the religion that inspired it. You can compare them with Housman when he saw the cherry tree and felt, 'I must fix that in a poem'. So the young Gothic architect, seeing existing cathedrals and feeling the excitement of them did not say, 'I must copy these cathedrals', but 'I must fix my delight in a cathedral and renew the joy, the intuition of the majesty of God'. And to get the delight he had to build still taller, and balance still greater weights on more slender pillars. For even those who love what they are given, the love, the delight, is always liable to fall away by familiarity. That is to say, the work of art, since it is realised in a symbol, in a thing, in stone, in words, has no life in itself. Its whole force is in its associations and these associations tend to lose power by familiarity. The prayer said every day tends to become a meaningless gabble, and the cathedral seen often tends to become a mere building. So churches invent new prayers to carry the old energy and architects invented Rheims to succeed Notre Dame.

But the second kind of original artist violently rebels against his teaching. He finds the existing art, the art he has been given, not merely too dull to express his feeling, but dead. He says of the Gothic he finds, not just, 'This is all right in its way, but not nearly exciting enough for what it is trying to mean', but 'This is just a heavy lump of stone which fails to mean anything. It is a fraud, a lie.'

He is so obsessed with his excitement that any existing work of art seems a treachery to the human spirit. To him, as to the scholar, with equally acute senses, what has been done, what we can call the aesthetic establishment, has an enormous, an overwhelming weight and bulk. But the scholar admires that bulk, its monumental dignity which throws so deep a shadow on his own sprouts of original fancy that they wither on the stem. What is more, as scholar, he has used all his imagination on the work of the past, he has written about it, he has made it his own. For him, it is a creation analysed, classified; he has reduced it to a conceptual order. For the obsessed man it is merely a vast and pompous edifice which stands between him and the people for whom, as he thinks, he has a highly important message.

And the very fact that scholars have classified and named its forms makes these forms irritating and boring to him. If he is an architect, he finds himself surrounded, not by original works of art, but by examples of classical, Queen Anne, Regency, Victorian style, labelled like specimens in bottles. In fact, he cannot see the buildings for the labels. He could no more express himself in any of these worn-out styles than the young Monet, burning with his intuition of a marvellous beauty in nature, could have painted an Ingres or a Corot.

And so he invents a completely new style, a new set of forms. He insists on flat roofs, horizontal windows in place of vertical, or complete glass walls, sliding doors; instead of building walls to hold up his interior, he makes an interior to hold up his walls. He abolishes all ornament and gets rid of the distinction of dining-room, drawing-room, kitchen—he runs them all together into one large irregular chamber. He rejects even the ideas of the past, its doctrine of formal design. He affirms that all these revolutionary changes are for use, according to Corbusier's formula that the house is a living machine. Beauty is of no account, all that matters is function.

He produces, that is, not only a new form of art, but a new theory to justify it. In fact, his new forms are largely emotive. They fulfil the same purpose as the ornamental details of the past. For many of them are actually less functional, less useful than the traditional. Horizontal windows are too low to see out of when you stand, too high when you sit, and they do not ventilate the upper part of a room. Glass walls in Britain mean enormously greater expense in heating, not to speak of cleaning. The large common-room sacrifices privacy, which is a fundamental need. The modern school of architecture has produced new beauty, a new monumental expression, but not any improvement in living convenience which cannot belong equally to the traditional. What the modern architect has really done is to revolt against forms of construction which have become so conventional, so conceptualised, that they are like the dead phrases which no poet can use again, clichés like the ambient air, the silver

56

stream, the vasty deep, the trackless wild. These have become conceptual forms, standard decoration, pieces of fustian, which actually hide the original intuition, true and powerful, of air, sea, and desert.

Thus, the artist's invention of new symbols is simply another aspect of the everlasting battle between the concept and the intuition. It is an attempt to overcome the primary defect of all concepts, all symbols, that they are mere things, that they live only by the associations we give them, and die by the same fate. For the effect of the architect's invention is that the old forms go out of date. It has become ridiculous to build a Greek concert hall or a Renaissance bank. These forms would express now not beauty but nonsense.

The old symbols are dead, and the new reign. But it is perfectly certain that the new will die in their turn of the same diseases.

XIII

THE MEANING OF THE SYMBOL

IN the last section we considered the problem of the original artist seeking a new form for his expression. This form, we saw, in architecture, was a new set of symbols which are highly arbitrary but will soon destroy the significance of the old.

All art uses the symbol. There is no other means by which one individual mind can express itself in material form and so communicate with another. For the writer, this form is language. By language the writer communicates both the fact and the feeling.

I know that language contains other elements as well as the symbol—signs, conjunctions, copulatives. But the symbol is its most important and even the signs can always become symbols. The word London on a map can mean for a motorist only a direction, but for someone who dreams of a career in London, an actor, a journalist, it provokes at once a complex of strong feelings. It becomes a powerful symbol, just as Big Ben, which for Westminster tells only the time, during the last war was a symbol for the whole world of endurance, of freedom, exciting very strong feelings of pride or hatred.

This war began almost entirely about symbols. The German people as individuals were as well off as any others, and actually possessed, relative to population, much more land than any of their neighbours. They had no dangerous enemies. All the surrounding peoples were extremely anxious for peace. But Hitler told the Germans they were dishonoured by defeat, betrayed by mysterious traitors, and threatened by their neighbours. He assured them that they were a master race and ought to rule Europe if not the world, that they ought to dare all things, and die, if necessary, for the glory of Germany. All this was symbolic language and it made the war. And symbolic language inspired much of the defence against Germany. I don't mean that freedom is not desirable for its own sake, that Britain was not fighting for a reality valuable in itself, but that the word, or symbol, had an immensely powerful effect, which could not have been obtained by a long and complex description of the democratic idea as it actually exists in Britain. Soldiers would not be especially excited to heroism by being told that they represented a free press, free arts, social justice, and so on. They would be apt to remember the exceptions. A course of recent history would produce a mere confusion in the soldier's mind, while the word 'freedom' has a certain definite impact, its emotional content. It calls up at once the idea of a general and very distinct difference between British economy, however complex, and the fascist or the Russian, with their ruthless censorship, their continuous will to control the minds of men, to turn them into puppets, robots, answering to the word of command from some political or religious boss.

I need not labour the symbolic power of a flag, of Church ritual, of the very shape of a church. We lately had a battle in the press about the new Coventry Cathedral. Was it to be a modern or a traditional building? The modernists said, 'Traditional Gothic is a bore, a worn-out convention. It has not only become boring, it conveys the idea of a Church that has lost all imagination, that is moribund.' The traditionalists argued that the new design was ugly, and looked more like a boot factory than a church.

Neither side seemed to perceive that the whole argument turned on the value of the symbol. The modernists were really saying, 'The symbolic form of the church, Gothic windows, tower and spire, has become worn-out and not only fails to convey a religious emotion, but merely excites boredom and contempt'. The traditionalists were saying, 'We have a symbolic architecture carrying the accumulated associations of a thousand years. Are we going to throw away such a precious and unique possession for a new form without any religious associations whatever?' Both sides, in short, had very good reasons, but what was really wanted at Coventry was what the church has had so often before, a new style, which refers to and recalls the old, as Early English referred to Norman and Perpendicular referred to Decorated, and yet had all the novelty, the excitement of the new creation. And possibly Coventry has it too; who knows till the thing is built.

We don't know yet if the creative art of our time can recreate the symbol we need in so important a department of our real life as that of religion. We need it because most of our life, the most important part, is expressed in symbols. Essentially we live in a symbolic world. The symbols, in their turn, affect our conduct. Think of the meaning and effect of uniform—why women, for whom it is a disaster, in ordinary dress, to meet each other in the same frock, take to uniform and are proud of it, as nurses, Wrens or Waafs. Why do women M.P.'s tend to a uniform attire of black and white, and why do men wear uniform in the evening while women carefully avoid it? Why do officers still carry ceremonial swords and judges wear wigs? Why do City men buy old thatched cottages? Such cottages have to be almost rebuilt, they are nearly always in damp valleys, so that the original peasants could get water, they are expensive to insure, and they need a new thatch every twenty years. All the same they have a high value in the estate market; that is, since the middle of the eighteenth century when Rousseau created the idea of the noble peasant living the simple life in communion with nature, preferably in a thatched cottage. For thatch, you see, is simpler than tiles or slates. It is made of reeds or straw, stuff which is grown in the earth. It is an important part of this symbol for a life of peace in the bosom of nature, it goes overhead, it encloses like a mother's arm. And Nature itself, as a word, in this context means, not the indifferent and often cruel enemy of mankind, familiar to us all, but Mother Nature, a loving providence desiring only to make all children happy and good.

The poets and dreamers of the romantic age invented a set of symbols still so powerful that the thatched cottage is not only at a premium in the estate market, it can actually bring the sense of relaxation, of peace, to the tired City man. It can make him feel that he is living in accord with something called Nature, and that he is therefore happier, better and more moral than if he inhabited a mere villa with damp-proof walls.

What's more, this set of symbols, idealising the simple life of the peasant, with his homespun and his handicrafts, descending through Ruskin to Gandhi, inspired millions in India to revolution, and may yet bring these millions to the real peasant's life, of poverty, squalor and superstition.

XIV

DIFFERENCE IN SYMBOLS

WHY did President Eisenhower refuse to wear a top hat at his inauguration? Because the top hat is a symbol meaning for the Americans an upper-class attitude, a certain formal dignity of manners, and a certain social discipline. The Republican managers argued that the common man in America hated all these things as an assumption of superiority, he wanted to feel equal with his President, he wanted to feel that his President was his own ordinary sort of person. Often, this sort of person is also a figment, it is what the Republican managers think that the common man thinks of himself. But it made a top hat into a symbol that could not be used. It is probably abolished for ever from American politics. Its fate is to have become, in America, too powerful a symbol. A universal fashion of the eighteen-fifties, when negro servants wore it in the slave market to show that they were respectable, trained butlers and footmen, coachmen and clerks—in short, to enhance their value—became in a hundred years the badge of the President-elect, and was then discarded because of its too great dignity. So the fashions of that time have become fancy dress with a thousand associations which they did not possess in their own time. Women's fashions of our own day expressing enterprise, gaiety, the joy of life, become in six months or so, dowdy, and in a year or two, meaningless, conveying nothing except the most depressing ideas of indifference to life, lack of enterprise or taste, poverty or obstinate conservatism. Their history, that is, is directly contrary to that of the top hat.

The new significant symbol becomes the insignificant bore or the ridiculous, even disgusting, folly. The cry all the time is for the new form, even when it is inconvenient: for lower car roofs, for skeleton arm-chairs made of wire, for couches with legs far from the corner, so that they tip up and throw you on the floor.

But because they are new they are expressive. They appear beautiful. They abolish the boredom of the conventional, and force the eye to observe the object, the actual thing. The new car, the wire arm-chair are new works of art, new symbols. The shape of the car, however inconvenient, symbolises speed, however slow the car. It relates it to the bird and the arrow. And this relation acts both ways. Works of art take symbolic associations from nature, nature from works of art.

Professor Empson, in his brilliant book *Seven Types of Ambiguity*, has analysed the line, 'Bare ruined choirs where late the sweet birds sang', to show the associations which give it such a rich beauty. But poetry also gives verbal associations to natural objects. In Nature, seen through the eyes of poets and novelists, the desert suggests the heroic traveller, the wild Arab, the hermit. The different seas all have references. The Atlantic gives an idea of gales and endurance, the Pacific of coral islands and sweet do-nothing. The word 'seaman' carries a quite different meaning from 'sailor', a tougher, more versatile and grimmer meaning. Mountains, once looked upon by travellers as mere dangerous nuisances, the haunt of brigands, are now symbols of the sublime. An Alp or an Himalayan peak, especially one not yet climbed, carries emotions formerly attached only to a religious shrine. Obvious associations are with the whiteness of snow, virgin snow, meaning purity, chastity and so related with vestal virgins, nuns; height connected with aloofness; danger related to awe and to the most primitive feelings about the gods, even the Christian God; remoteness connected with the transcendent. If you add the word or idea of the untrodden, you get further emotions belonging to the religious shrine, the sacred place. You may say that there is no logical passage from mountain slopes that are untrodden only because the explorer has not yet reached them, to a holy place, untrodden because it is forbidden and barred off. But in this realm of the symbol, we move always close to, or within, the reasoning of a dream, the psychology of association; not merely in some exceptional experience such as a visit to Switzerland or Kashmir, but always and all the time. The most ordinary sentence in the newspaper, or last week's thriller, carries meanings for us which are fully operative, but of which we do not detect the workings because they are subconscious. We can often, if we care to do so, bring them to the surface and analyse at least some part of them, but normally we accept them and suffer them without inquiry.

Consider this sentence: he left the room. And compare it with: he departed into the street. They have entirely different associations, and a novelist might hesitate between them. The first is the simplest possible means of relating a fact. It uses deliberately, therefore, the most general terms and they convey the fact, according to the context, that the movement has no special significance. The second—using a charged word, like 'departed', with a hundred associations from Watteau to the departure platform, to the eternal partings of a hundred romances; and 'street'—is full of dramatic emphasis and belongs to a more emotive context. Of course, in each case, the context will profoundly affect the meaning. The first phrase could have the more powerful emphasis of a sudden change of tone, a quite flat statement in a charged background. The second could be over-emphasis, comical, derisory, or mannered. But this only enforces my point, that the simplest words carry a weight of meaning by association, and that the meaning is highly subjective. Yet the two sentences remain quite distinct in themselves. The first is always simple, flat, general; the second dramatic and charged. It is only because they have a meaning in themselves that they can be used to carry other meanings in the general mood of the book. You can play down the first as you choose, or use it for emphasis, but in each case, its value to you depends on its quality. Words as symbols have flexible connotations, but their meanings are definite within a context. Consider the word 'street'. It is always different from 'road'. 'On the streets' is completely different from 'on the roads'. Fleet Street, Wall Street, Downing Street, have large applications but do not merge into each other. Baldwin's pipe has a quite different effect from Churchill's cigar. Both were powerful symbols, important factors in the careers of these statesmen. They suggested moral qualities that could not have been expressed so cogently or directly by any other means. The pipe stood for honesty, the simple *sans façon* of the plain country man, a very useful disguise for a subtle, intelligent, sophisticated but lazy statesman. But it always carried quite different implications from a cigarette. Only a hostile caricaturist would

66

portray an ambitious politician smoking a cigarette. It connotes lightness of mind, even decadence. Yet the cigar which is, in caricatures, the
symbol of the ruthless plutocrat, the oppressor of
the poor, in Churchill's mouth expresses a hundred admirable and popular qualities, such as
vitality, love of life, defiance of popular opinion,
independence of mind, together with all sorts of
fine shades in allusion, according to the personal
idea. That is to say, it has become amenable to a
context; but this does not mean that it has the
same value as the pipe. On the contrary, it belongs to a completely different set of symbols
where its importance is due to its quite different
associations. To see the difference, think of Baldwin with a cigar, Churchill with a pipe.

XV

IMPRESSIONISTS

WE are so accustomed to this symbolic
world in which the most important part of
our lives, the emotional, is passed, that we
do not notice its arbitrary nature.

We are told that a British envoy once took a
Gainsborough to China: a mandarin, of high culture,
admired the work, but asked, 'Why is it the custom
in England for ladies to have one side of their faces
so dirty?' And it was extremely difficult to make him
believe that this brown dirt on the painted faces was

a device to give the illusion of shadow and a three-dimensional form.

We are surprised at the mandarin; but not at the critics who told the world that Monet's paintings were daubs without sense or form, that Renoir could not paint. Here is Albert Wolff, critic of *Le Figaro*, on the first Impressionist Exhibition of 1875:

These so-called artists call themselves members of the uncompromising set, or impressionists. Seizing hold of canvases, colours and brushes, they daub a few tones haphazard and sign their names underneath! In a similar manner, at Ville-Évrard, lunatics pick up pebbles from the roadway and imagine that they have found diamonds. A terrible spectacle of human vanity straying to the borderland of madness....But try to explain to M. Renoir that the torso of a woman is not a mass of flesh in a state of decomposition, with green and violet patches which denote a complete state of cadaveric putrefaction.... You might as well waste your time in explaining to one of Dr Blanche's patients, who thinks he is the Pope, that he really lives in Batignolles and not at the Vatican.

And here is Roger Ballu, in *La Chronique des Arts et de la Curiosité*, on Renoir in 1877:

In *La Balançoire* and *Le Bal du Moulin de la Galette* the same M. Renoir set himself the task of copying nature servilely. One's first impression is that some accident must have happened to his pictures on their way from his studio to the exhibition. For they are spotted with round marks, with here and there what look like stripes. However, in examining them carefully we begin to see what their author wanted to do—he tried to render the effect of full sunlight pouring through

68

foliage on to people sitting under the tree. The round marks are supposed to be the shadows cast by each leaf —a truly impressive feat, I must confess. But on undertaking such a struggle with nature, do we not expose ourselves to an inexcusable and senseless defeat, for the very good reason that such an undertaking will never be anything save ridiculous.

Wolff has been called an ignorant and blind fool without taste, without even the power to understand the aesthetic qualities he wrote about so glibly. Actually he was in precisely the same position as the mandarin. He had before him a set of symbols, a symbolic form that he could not interpret. It gave him no coherent and appropriate feeling. Wolff, in short, was a highly cultivated man and a very good critic within the limits of his education. But that conceptual education which made him a good judge of all French schools to that date, and especially the current school in the tradition of Ingres, David and the late Corot, also made it impossible for him to comprehend a new symbolic system, a new intuition. For to him they were frauds. And so the critics of any time, the good, the honest, the informed critics, will always hate and despise an original artist or writer. At best, they try to put him into one of their pigeon-holes. They say of his book 'This is the school of James, although rather inferior; this is bad Conrad'. At worst they rage against him. And the rage often hides a fear. For they know what has happened to critics before. They have seen them, probably in their own lifetime, become absurd with the art which they judged, the only art they could judge.

Original writers and artists, men like Cézanne or Lawrence, are lucky if they are not damned out of hand, if they are only traduced or misunderstood.

The Impressionists were highly original. They had found the new exciting intuition of nature as light and pure colour, and they had invented a new technique to express it. So they were faced by a world which not only failed to understand this new language, but violently hated it. However, like all evangelists convinced of truth, they would rather have starved, they did sometimes starve, rather than abandon their expression of that truth, their message to the world. Gradually they were understood and appreciated by other young people, suffering from the boredom of the old accepted system and delighted to find a new expression. Gradually they prevailed, until the old school of the salons could not sell a picture or make a living, till those carefully educated, highly intelligent and skilful artists of the previous age were absolutely scorned as mere scene-painters.

But in their turn, towards the end of the century, the Impressionists began to be despised, a new fashion came in and just as the Impressionist masters had revolted against Bougereau and Meissonnier, so the Fauves despised the Impressionists as mechanical and brainless imitators of natural effects—illusionists. After the Fauves, of course, we have had the abstract school, now staggering to its doom.

XVI

FORM OF THE SYMBOL

THE symbol, the symbolic system is not only arbitrary, it is highly fragile. It is always dying. Fashions in art, in literature, are little more enduring than those of dress. Kant is superseded by Hegel, Hegel by Schopenhauer, and in our day, Bergson, who was the craze of 1910, gives place to Wittgenstein, who is or has been the inspiration of the nineteen-forties. A symbolic system of any kind quickly becomes ineffective, a bore. Why? The reason, I think, is due not only to the decay of the symbol itself, a mere thing dependent for its effectiveness on our response to its associations, but to the same conflict between concept and intuition which bedevils the artist at work. The symbol as thing, word, gesture, ballet-step, building, is a compound of concept and associations. A cathedral, a flag, like any other work of art is the product of conceptual thought designed to convey emotion by the associations attached to its form. But as a mere thing, it requires to have its associations renewed. It tends always to lose them and to sink into the empty object, the bare concept-label, the mechanical sign or gesture. The word becomes a word from a dictionary. The brush stroke, the style, of a painter becomes by repetition a term in his expression, analogous to a word. It is part of his language. He always makes that statement in that form. The new

71

critics learn that language and teach it to the public. Pretty soon the public is seeing, not a revelation of the real, but a fine example of So-and-so with all his characteristic tricks; and especially the new generation, taught the new language, see only the specimens, constructs in that language, and not the revelation. For the revelation has been made. The world has been illuminated for them. The illumination has become common daylight. They can all see with the eyes of the established school, whatever it is, and do not find anything wonderful in it. It has lost that miraculous effect of the new truth.

It may be said that the demand for the new is simply a mark of youth; that the love of the old is that of age. But the love of the old arises directly from the same situation. It belongs directly to the symbolic world, of created works of art. As we saw, everyone, from childhood, creates his own idea of things and realises, so far as possible, his own desires according to that idea. He makes a world that is his work of art. He is not only expressed in it, he is committed to it, and its destruction is for him an irreparable loss, for with it he loses all the meaning, all the emotional satisfaction of his life, its whole realisation.

This realisation consists, not only of religious and political belief, of patriotism, often of various pseudo-national myths, a total valuation of life, but of aesthetic taste, expressed in everything that a man acquires: dress, his home, his books, his pictures, his furniture. None of these things may be, in actual fact, different from the common type. Most of them are selected in the first place because they conform to a type. The young married couple take a villa in a row of exactly similar villas and furnish it with mass-produced new furniture from the local store. The man buys a suit to conform to the current fashion. Yet in a very short time that villa and its furniture will have come to seem unique to that couple. The house is their home, the furniture their first furniture. It will acquire associations and give them thereby special pleasure, richer impressions. Any council engaged in slum-clearance will tell you of the difficulty and often the danger of moving old people out of some squalid tenement into a convenient new house in the new suburb. The people hate to be moved, they may literally die of it. In the new surroundings they don't want to live any longer because life has lost its meaning for them. And any wife knows the difficulty of removing her husband from an old coat. It has come, in its rags, to represent for him leisure, rest, peaceful enjoyment, in the garden, or an arm-chair. He does not feel the same peace except in that coat.

All our love of the old is based on such association, or on sympathetic association as created by the art of the time. Old buildings, antique furniture, have about them the associations of history, of period, as given to us by the historians and novelists. They are enriched symbols of the past suggesting to us

73

all the various stories connected with them, the idea of the men and women who have suffered with them. This passion for the old is an analogue of our own love of our own things, not because they are possessions, but because they are part of that world that we have created for ourselves, and, like any creative artist, we have a special pleasure in what we have made. What's more, as I say, we are committed to it. The reason why the young revolutionary becomes the old conservative is not some disease of age, but simply the fact that he has created in imagination that world, a free revolutionary world, which is being torn from him. We live in the creation and it presents us with two kinds of tragedy: that of the young genius who desires to create his own new world, in politics or in art, and is defeated by the academicism of those whose art and reputations are threatened by his innovation; and that of the conservative whose world is being destroyed.

XVII

STYLE

MANY young rebels, young geniuses are defeated. As for the tragedy of the old, it is even more common. I remember myself at sixteen, on a holiday in France, seeing an artist of my acquaintance in a garden. He was a man over sixty, who had at one time been hung, year after year, in the Academy. He painted chiefly girls in gardens. I had gone to the farmhouse where he lived with his ragged family and an exhausted wife, and I had found him standing among the hollyhocks beside an easel on which he had placed his latest picture, in a new gilt frame. It had just been returned to him after rejection by the Academy. He had now been rejected four or five years in succession—he could not sell his pictures any longer and was in deepest poverty. Apparently he had brought out this picture to compare his painted flowers with the real ones. He was standing all alone at this task when I arrived to fetch a basket of eggs.

He asked me to look at the picture, to agree with him about the excellence of the painting. He pointed out some of the best touches and said, 'But they don't want good work at the Academy, or anywhere else. They don't care for beauty any more. They hate it. They only want this new rubbish. The world has gone mad—it despises beauty and only wants ugliness.' And then he began to cry. I'd never seen a man of that age in tears, and I was greatly upset. I murmured some words of consolation—that I thought the picture was very good and didn't know why it had been rejected—and escaped as soon as I could.

Of course, I did not even comprehend the full despair of this unhappy man. I was all for the Impressionists. I was amusing myself on a school holiday with Impressionism, and I believed that there was no other really valid art. As I came away, I thought, 'Poor old man, but why did he ever become a painter? He could never have done anything worth-while—his pictures are ridiculous in their high finish, mere photographic illustrations fit for a Christmas supplement.'

The tragedy here is that I could not even understand the tragedy thus offered to me, of a man of sixty, not only ruined financially, but whose whole life and skill had lost its meaning.

This tragedy is taking place all the time, in all the arts, but at varying rates of speed and depth. You would expect a change of fashion, of style, of symbolic system, to take place roughly in the period of a generation, about twenty-five years; because it is the new generation, or the more enterprising and intelligent part of it, which demands always a new statement, a new form, or rather a new intensity and immediacy of expression. As we saw, the very completeness of a conceptual education produces, in certain highly sensitive temperaments, reaction and revolt. It promises too little or too much. Tolstoy revolted against Church and State because of his highly dogmatic education. It spoke of ideal Christian love, of the Kingdom of Heaven on earth, and Tolstoy, with his brothers, dreamed of bringing such a world to pass. His brother Nicholas told him of the green stick, on which was written the secret by which men may cease to suffer or quarrel and by which the whole world could live in brotherhood and peace. This green stick and its message made so deep an impression on Tolstoy that when he died nearly seventy years later, he chose to be buried in the place where it was supposed to lie. And so the impression made on Tolstoy by his education in the tenets of the Orthodox Church caused him to turn against that very Church when he grew up. For he happened to be more impressionable than the average.

The young Wordsworth and Coleridge, the young Keats, because they loved poetry, rebelled against the traditional poetry. It is typically the most intelligent and sensitive of the young who become revolutionaries, destroyers.

The change of fashion, of style in literature is rarely so frequent and complete as that of the plastic arts. But this, I suspect, is due simply to art schools which teach a new method to thousands as soon as it becomes accepted. The consequence is that hordes of art students, taught it as a mere technique, practise it as a mere method, vulgarise it, and within a few years present their contemporary art-public with work already purely mechanical and imitative. This produces the inevitable reaction; the young revolt more quickly and seek more urgently a true expressive form for their own new intuition.

It is true, of course, that literature is taught to whole populations, but it is not taught as a technique for expression, as a set of tricks for mere show. It will be interesting to see if the writing schools in the United States produce there a more rapid decay in

77

symbolic system, a more rapid turnover in literary fashion.

I seem here to contradict the argument of Section 11 that a factual and conceptual education in technical method was probably the best, and perhaps the only effective method of instruction for the practical artist and writer; what's more, that it was impossible for a good teacher not to have his own prejudices and impart them, for without prejudice he will have no convictions, impart no enthusiasms. But acquisition of a style, even under another's influence, is not the same thing as the assumption of a set of tricks by the student. Stevenson has misled a great many young writers by his statement that he learnt his art by playing the sedulous ape, by imitating the masters. Stevenson as a writer did himself infinite damage by inventing for himself a style before he had decided what he was going to do with it. A style assumed as a style lies over everything like the celebrated Brown Gravy which so offended Brillat-Savarin. It is a form that cannot possibly cohere in the writer's content; it is a set of tricks. But the student who accepts the style of a teacher because it seems to him to express an important intuition is so far enabled to be sincere, even if he ends up as merely the subordinate member of a school. This is the fate of the very large percentage of students in all the arts, and I do not know any certain way by which it can be avoided; for every student must have a form of expression, and he must

78

learn it by a purely technical and conceptual education. That education will always be in conflict with his power of intuition, of knowing objects, of knowing minds, of recognising situations as they are; and any attempt to escape from that dilemma by the invention of some artificial difference, some merely showy style, will be even more ruinous in producing a fundamental split between the form and the content.

XVIII

INTUITION AND CONCEPT

THERE is in fact no escape from this fundamental conflict of intuition and concept, and from the fragility of the symbol. All symbols and symbolic systems must die, and their life tends to grow shorter as art education improves and the arts grow richer.

You may ask in that case why libraries and galleries are full of the masterpieces of the past, all of them in exploded symbols, why do we still enjoy Jane Austen and Gainsborough, though we cannot and do not want to write Jane Austen or paint Gainsborough. This was itself a puzzle to me until some years ago when I inherited a picture, a family conversation-piece. I had known for forty years that I was to get it, and I had asked myself many times what I could do with that fearful Victorian picture when it arrived. My walls were fully occupied with

79

good modern work, yet I could not hang this picture, a family picture, in the back-passage, or put it in the attic to deteriorate.

But when the picture arrived at last, and I unpacked it, it struck me as remarkably good. The more I looked at it the more I was impressed. I turned out an excellent still life by Meninsky to give it a good place. Sir John Rothenstein, of the Tate, calling to see some of my latest acquisitions, noticed this picture and remarked on its quality. He said, 'That is the kind of thing the Victorians excelled in. See how the painter is completely devoted to his subject. There is no egotism anywhere in the statement, he is not hoping someone will say, "a typical specimen of So-and-so", he is simply trying to give us the essence of the scene.' I quite agreed with Sir John, but still I was not satisfied, until one day it struck me that the picture I was looking at was completely different from the picture I had first seen in 1916, forty years before. From a contemporary portrait, or rather a portrait only a few years out-of-date, of two ladies and a child, the ladies in fashions which had just become ridiculous, in a room whose furniture had lately become demoded, the picture was changed into a period piece. Added to its effect was all that had been felt and written about the Victorian age by historians, by novelists, in those forty years. Thus the whole mass of associations belonging to that picture and to the late Victorian style in which it was painted had become, not only

80

enormously enlarged, but formalised within the idea of a period. This idea, the idea of a period and its character is, of course, also the creation of art. And as soon as it acquires a form and a meaning, it has a very powerful supercharge of value, not only aesthetic but general. It affects political and historical thought, the whole form of men's minds.

This is not the place to discuss the validity of such an idea—or its relation with fact, but it is worth while to notice that its truth, if any, is aesthetic rather than comprehensive. The eighteenth century, for instance, in the idea, is rational, deist, ceremonious, highly cultivated. It rejected humanitarian sentiment and a personal God as illusions of plebeian self-deception. Its manners were exquisite as its judgment was cool and frank. But, in fact, there were countless editions of Bunyan in the eighteenth century, the evangelists flourished. Richardson, that sentimentalist, made a European reputation, and Rousseau in France is credited with dissolving the Bourbon monarchy in a flood of tears. Manners among a large section of the working class were inconceivably brutal, as Wesley shows us, and London was a sink.

All the same, the idea of a highly civilised culture is so strong in us that eighteenth-century dress at any fancy-dress ball stands for the grace of life. So too crinoline in fancy-dress means for us the qualities imposed upon mid-Victorian chaos by a hundred artists and writers from Leach to G. M. Young.

And in my picture, my aunt's hat of 1897 carried for me by itself a whole formal and moral implication which it could not possess when it was new, and which was completely contrary to that which it had had when I first saw it as an absurd object. It had regained the dignity of a monument.

So the works of the past come back to us in a different context. No one has ever seen the *Hamlet* that Shakespeare wrote and that the Elizabethans enjoyed. No one, in fact, reads the same book or sees the same picture twice. These differences from day to day are not noticeable or important, but from century to century they are enormously important and I suggest that one of their important effects is precisely in the reincarnation of a symbolic system. Victorian technique is still Victorian, and it expresses the Victorian idea of an artist's character and his individual Victorian world. But the system itself, having become a set of tricks and a bore, having fallen into contempt, and having been abandoned even by the Academy and the critics, has acquired, merely by the passage of time, all the charm of novelty. It is no longer subject to imitation and therefore it has acquired all the virtue of a unique and original attitude towards the world, a virtue it lacked in its own time. It is no longer a specimen of popular exploitation. And as period work it has had added to it an immense significance from all that we now imagine about the Victorians.

The great art of the past, in fact, becomes greater

all the time, richer in significance. This does not, of course, allay the tragedy of the artist who is outmoded. I dare say that painter I knew whose girls in gardens had become unsaleable, would now find his pictures once more in high esteem. The very completeness of the Victorian style which damned them in 1906, would make them the more significant and desirable in 1956. But this painter is dead long ago. And if his pictures survive, they are probably sitting frameless in the attics of the junk shops. Frameless because a gilt frame has an intrinsic value: I once saw a room full of frameless canvases, all by distinguished Academicians. There was, for instance, a Leader, eight by six, for sale at thirty shillings. It had cost some collector at least a thousand pounds; the gilt frame had fetched three or four.

I don't know if Leader will ever return to us as a great master. I shouldn't dare to dogmatise about any painter. I can't admire Leader myself—I belong to a time of reaction against the Victorians. But whether he comes back or not, the tragedy remains that artists, especially painters, are apt to live much longer than their style, than their symbols. A man of eighty has outlived probably three new schools of painting, two of architecture and poetry, a hundred in dress.

XIX

EXPLORATION AND CONSTRUCTION

ALL symbols fade and die by use. They lose their emotional force and value. Words are gradually deprived of their harmonics. Names take the place of actual events, so that a tourist seeing London gets no reaction from Westminster Abbey except the reflection, 'I can now tick that off'; a reaction all the more likely when he has been seeing churches for a week past.

The symbol, in short, like the concept, to which it continually approximates, is also the enemy of the intuition. The moment the artist expresses his intuition in any formal terms, this expression tends to destroy for him the force of his intuition.

I said that, in spite of Croce, the most vivid and continuous experience of all artists is the gap between their intuition and its expression, and all great artists, all great writers, seek continually to overcome it. It's quite easy for any experienced painter or writer to avoid that troublesome problem and use his technical skill to write or paint works which do not attempt to express any intuition at all, but merely imitate some master who has done so. This process, as we saw, is one chief reason for the destruction of each symbolic system in turn, the imitation by hordes of students of what was once an original and expressive creation.

But the great master is perpetually concerned with

intuition. It is his primary task to keep in touch with it, that is to say, with the real. Dostoevsky, in *The Brothers Karamazov*, wrecked his whole plan of showing the superiority of the orthodox dogma over Ivan's atheistic attack by giving Ivan the most crushing arguments. That means that when he asked himself how would Ivan see reality, how would he argue about it, he realised with the force of intuition a truth that had been before only the statement of a hypothetic case, and then expressed it, with the utmost power. So that his scheme for that chapter, his concept *a priori* of what that chapter would mean, was completely ruined.

And we saw how Tolstoy sat impatiently trying to find out exactly what his feeling, his intuition, was.

So all great artists are preoccupied, as if by nature, with reality. They assume, from the beginning, that it is their task to reveal a truth about some permanent and fundamental real. The problem of the conflict between the concept and the intuition is always with them. And it is not enough to describe the intuition in words, it has to be given in the work of art.

For the novelist, in fact, there is not only a huge gap between intuition and concept, the first raw statement, but between that statement and its working out in a story, a fable. It is easy for a philosopher, seeking a harmonious whole, to say that the two last processes are the same, that having expressed the situation for himself, the artist has taken the essential step—that he has his work of art and that any further operation is simply recording. This is simply not true in professional experience.

For the truth is that the work of art as completely realised is the result of a long and complex process of exploration, as well as construction. This is true even of a painter. The notion that a painter suddenly imagines a composition expressive of his feeling and straightway puts it down, is untrue. He begins with a general idea, no doubt—if he has a landscape before his eyes, he wants to express his feeling about that landscape in colour and form. But he has not yet got colour and form on canvas, he has not translated the actual fields and trees into symbols and, however experienced he is, he does not know exactly how to get the effect he wants, or even if it is possible within the limits of his material. He proceeds by trial and error. Watch him at work. He is not only uncertain of the exact effect of separate touches, he is still more uncertain of the result of their contrast and conjunction. And the more experienced he is, the more accomplished and subtle, the more care he will take. Manet would scrape off his paint day after day until, after fifty trials, he could satisfy himself that no further improvement was possible. That is, he was not merely expressing an intuition, he was continually discovering new possibilities in his own work, now become objective to him, and realising them. The whole process was one of exploration as well as expression.

This is true of all the arts. Poets gradually construct both their verse and their meaning by continued test and alteration; novelists discover new aspects of their theme, and also new limitations of their technique, as they work.

I was once sitting at tea with that great artist and brilliant technician, Miss Compton-Burnett, and she said, 'Mr Cary, I have been wondering when your novel is to be published. I saw it advertised at least a year ago, but it doesn't seem to be out yet'. I said that I had run into difficulties; the novel had indeed taken nearly three years. But I thought it was nearly finished because when I changed it for the better in one place, I found I had damaged it in some other. Miss Compton-Burnett answered me at once, 'I know exactly what you mean. It happens to me too. At a certain point my novels set. They set just as hard as that jam jar. And then I know they are finished.' That is to say, the writing of a novel is not only the exploration of a theme, of character, of possibility, but of technical limits.

When Proust was writing his masterpiece he had a letter from Mme Schiff to complain that he had made Swann ridiculous. Proust answered that he had had no wish to make Swann ridiculous, far from it. But when he had come to this part of the work, he had found it unavoidable. That is to say, he had been compelled by the logic of the craft to do what he had not intended or imagined himself doing. For if he had not made Swann ridiculous, the whole work

would have suffered. I don't know to what passage
Mme Schiff referred, but I have supposed it was
to Swann's jealousy. Now without jealousy Swann
would lose much of his actuality for us: much,
therefore, of our sympathy: and the whole book
would lose enormously by this failure in one of its
major characters. And jealousy that makes a man
ridiculous is all the more authentic, all the more (as
we say, truly) real. It belongs to the world of real
passions, and, in Swann, conveys us into that world.

XX

EXPRESSION AND COMMUNICATION

THIS discovery of Proust's that Swann, in spite
of Proust's own intention, had got to be
ridiculous, is like Dostoevsky's discovery that
Ivan Karamazov as a realised character had more
powerful arguments than Dostoevsky had allowed
for in his plot. It is a form of intuition; it is the
immediate recognition of a real truth, a penetration
into the realities of character. And it has broken
through Proust's first conception of Swann, and
immediately deepened his awareness of Swann's
possibilities. Swann, as a character created by
Proust, here assumes an individual personality, to
be intuited by his own author. Of course, this interpretation of Swann is due largely to factors which
are beyond Proust's control, I mean the nature of

88

humanity itself. If you invent a man, a person, he has to behave like a person, and, as Tolstoy said, psychology is the one thing an author must not invent.

But the genius of Proust was active both in the realisation of Swann's potentiality, in the decision to make him ridiculous, and in the power to adapt the general form of his work to this unforeseen development. For this he required technical invention, experience and dexterity.

Tolstoy said that the difference between great writing and small writing is in the minute details. I think this is true, if by minute details he meant such significant details as Swann's ridiculous conduct in jealousy. And I think he could have added that most of these details are devised during the process of the work, that for the great writer nothing is settled until he has explored all the possibilities of his characters and his theme.

Thus the gap between the writer and his material remains throughout his work. What he has completed becomes at once for him objective, and at once therefore something to be explored. He explores it from two points of view: as artist, to know its possibilities of development; as critic, to know if it has had the effect he intended. For like the painter, he never knows exactly the effect of what he has created, until he has tested it as observer.

This does not mean, of course, that the artist, the writer, should have what is called the public in view, that he should attempt to be comprehensible to any special persons. For one thing, the public in this sense does not exist, it is a figment like the average man. No one can say what this mysterious being will understand.

A writer who finds himself incomprehensible to critics and public may say, 'This is a failure on my part—I meant to be understood'. But I doubt very much if he can compromise without insincerity.

I'm not talking here about writers who try to produce the best-sellers. They are in quite another category. They are producing something to sell, they are necessarily imitators and they can't take much interest in the truth. If they did, they might be unpopular. A writer like Dickens may indeed sell, but that was not because he attempted to give the public what he thought it would like, but because what he himself liked to do was also liked by a great number of people. He had the good fortune to find himself doing a popular thing. But he is a rare case. And it is rarer still for an original writer to be a best-seller—at least till he is dead. For the very reason that he is original he is bound to be misunderstood by critics and read by few. He will be lucky to be published at all. What is remarkable about the career of D. H. Lawrence is not that so brilliant a book as *The Rainbow* took so long to find a publisher, but that it was published at all, and received, even in Lawrence's lifetime, some appreciation.

The struggle to be read, the hatred which his work

excited when it was published at last, embittered Lawrence. And this is the common case of the original artist. He wants not only to express his unique idea of things, but to communicate it. He is, in fact, almost invariably a propagandist, he is convinced that his idea of things is true and important and he wants to convert others, he wants to change the world.

This is true not only of the great Russians, of Dickens, Thackeray, George Eliot, Wells, Kipling, Conrad, Galsworthy, but of men like Gide and Proust. Proust's cry is very simple, 'Give us more truth, more sincerity, more people like Swann, like my grandmother. Let me rest in peace and the security of affection.'

It is no shame to the original writer that he wants to be read, to communicate, and we know that the ambition can be present to a first-class writer. The desire to be understood may even frustrate genius. Katherine Mansfield abandoned the writing of a novel because, she said, it had ceased to look like a novel. That is to say, she had in mind a public that was accustomed to a certain form of construction, and she felt that it would not accept her work as a novel. She was too modest to say, 'I'll write my own kind of novel and let them take it if they can'.

But this was what she ought to have done. For an original writer must not expect appreciation. No one can blame Lawrence for his anger against the public and critics of his day. We read with astonishment the kind of attacks made upon him and wonder that such crass meanness of spirit and blindness of taste could exist in what was supposed to be a civilised people. But in fact all that was wrong with those critics was that they belonged to their time, and they were not prepared to recognise an original writer. What they wanted was new specimens of the contemporary school, derivations and imitations of Galsworthy, Wells, James; the false originality of the clever fellow who takes up a current fashion and gives it a new turn.

Lawrence could not have pleased these critics without ceasing to be Lawrence, without throwing away his genius. It would not only have been useless, it would have been a hopeless enterprise for him to attempt to be understood by them. It would have been equally wrong and impossible for him to write without the desire to be comprehensible. For the writer has a meaning to communicate, that meaning is the order, the form of his work, and unless it is communicated, he does not know that it is there.

But since it is his own meaning, it is no good for him to ask any other person if he has communicated it. He has to be his own critic. The writer's test of success in creating an ordered form is, 'Does it mean to me what I want it to mean?' He communicates with himself because he can't at that stage communicate with anyone else.

To do this he treats the work again as external to himself, as objective, as fact from direct experience.

He asks only, 'What have I got? What have I done?'
I am speaking as a professional when I say that the
great difficulty here is not only to see the objective
clearly as it is, to value your achievement with an
unprejudiced eye, but to know what it is all about.
You are faced with a mass of words, and a story like
many other stories, your characters and your general
theme. But what is the meaning of it all, the real
meaning? Where is the exciting discovery with which
you started? That is to say, where is your revelation?

What makes this problem even more difficult is
that the intuition was probably a very simple and
common one. For all the primary and important
dramas and situations in life are extremely common
and ordinary. The majority of all novels, plays and
films are about love, the situation of boy meets girl.
Love is the theme of the greatest as well as the
cheapest, for it is one of the most important things
that ever happen to nine-tenths of men and women.
For them it is no cliché, and it should be a primary
intuition of the novelist. But how is he to keep the
freshness of that intuition for months while handling
the situation common to millions of popular novels
and all the magazines?

XXI

EXPERIENCE AND WORD

THERE is a highly illuminating story about Henry James. Writing about *The Spoils of Poynton* he tells us that what he calls the germ, what I call the intuition, for the book, came to him at a luncheon-party where his next-door neighbour told him of a family quarrel which had caused the break-up of a household. This house, the woman said, had been a work of art, beautifully furnished and arranged, but now the furniture was to be scattered.

This was James's germ. And one can understand why. For James, the final tragedy of the world was the fragility of all goodness, all beauty, all excellence. For him, the innocent, the honest, the sincere, the fine were, on that very account, specially liable to be destroyed.

This was his theme from that minor masterpiece, *Daisy Miller* to *Portrait of a Lady* and *The Wings of the Dove*. In *The Death of the Lion* we have the destruction of a fine genius by the imbecilities of society hostesses amusing themselves, and in *The Spoils of Poynton* the ruin of a unique work of art; a house furnished in so harmonious a manner that it makes a complete whole, a complete aesthetic experience. Henry James discovered, in the gossip of his luncheon partner about a very common thing, the break-up of a family household, an intuition so strong and profound that it set him to the long and troublesome task of a whole novel. From that intuition he made a masterpiece. The significant part of the story for me is that in recording the incident, his discovery of the germ, he complains that the wretched woman would go on talking. This comment has amused people with the idea that Henry James was simply bored, but to the professional writer it has a quite different and much deeper meaning. The difficulty of the artist, the writer, having got his intuition, his revelation, is to hold on to it; it is, as I say, usually a very simple thing and often extremely common, it has been recorded thousands of times in common speech. It has taken a conceptual form in words, and the words, especially the common words that record the break up of a masterpiece or falling in love or any other fundamental revelation, are so worn by use that they have lost all impact. What does love mean in the newspaper or the ordinary story? It is a word which strikes on the mind merely as a label, the flattest kind of concept. Thus it actually hides the truth behind; a powerful and unique emotion disappears behind a word which has by itself almost no emotional impact. When Henry James was indignant with that woman, his innocent luncheon partner who would go on talking after, by accident, she had given him his germ, his intuition, he was terrified that he would lose it again, that he would forget it. He knew that it is the easiest thing in the world to do so. For, the moment he had translated his intuition into an idea, into words, his excited feeling of discovery began to leak away, and the idea began to seem dull, commonplace, and to supersede the intuition.

In all the arts the great problem of the artist is to preserve the force of his intuition, his germ, what is sometimes called his inspiration, throughout the long process of technical construction. For most of that technical construction is conceptual. The writer, faced with a problem of expression, calls up all his experience, and the greater part of that experience is recorded conceptually and must be so. He asks himself to start with, 'What characters shall I need? What kind of leading character? What background? What general scheme?' Even if he does not design a plot to begin with, he forms, and has to form, a general idea of the working-out in action of his choice of characters. Here, of course, he is faced with another gap, never acknowledged by the philosopher: that between form and content. We are always told that they are inseparable, but this is true only in the art of philosophy. For the writer the situation is very much more complex. He has to deal with language which consists, it is true, of forms which are also contents. That is to say, they are meanings. On the other hand he has his intuition, the emotional experience that he wishes to convey in all its original force. This is to be the content of his book, but when he gets to work he has to ask himself how the manipulation of words, themselves already charged with meaning, will convey this other larger meaning which is to be his content. And when he has put them together in scenes conceptually devised to convey this content, he has to ask himself if they do so; that is to say, he has, on the one hand, a set of forms, and on the other hand, the content which he wishes to convey. He is of course actually comparing two contents, that of the forms he has on the page and that of the content he has in his imagination. But in this comparison, the first set of forms, the symbols on the page, have a double aspect: that of their content, as symbols, sentence by sentence and page by page, and that of their total effect.

This distinction is again a fundamental experience for the writer, and he must make it. He must not tell himself that since form and content are the same, and all the separate sentences give the right meaning, therefore the total meaning must be present. This is very easy to do. For, as I said, a writer as his own first reader and critic has special difficulties in achieving detachment. He knows that he is apt to be over-critical, and so to throw away a first draft simply because it has become boring to him.

It saves immense trouble to say, 'All the details are right, therefore the whole thing must be right'. But it is absolutely fatal to the work.

For instance, from my own experience, I wrote the railway station chapter in *Prisoner of Grace* to show how the husband, by certain suggestions, makes it impossible for his wife to carry on with her elopement. She just daren't run away from him. This scene was in the first person. Afterwards, for reasons I need not explain here, I began the book in the third person. The dialogue in the railway station scene was, of course, precisely the same, word for word. But it did not convince any more. For the reader is aware subconsciously that he is now dealing with a third-person narrative. And so he cannot give the same credence to the wife's descriptions of her own feelings. He knows that the author needs the woman's change of mind for his plot, and the author in a third-person narrative is always present at the back of the reader's mind. So the whole content, the meaning of the chapter was altered without the alteration of a single word in it.

How did I know that the content was changed? Because I had fixed somewhere in my memory the content, the meaning I wanted to give.

XXII

THE TOTAL SYMBOL

THIS content fixed in the memory seems to be the direct impact of the intuition, which stands for record. It can be obscured, overlain, but it remains, otherwise there would be no good in the artist's attempts to get back to it. The cherry tree which Housman gave us in his poem was the cherry tree as intuition found it in his memory, before he attempted to express it in words. For all intuitions, being the work of the subconscious, are first recorded in the memory, they are in the first place automatic reactions to the outside actuality or some real element in it.

A very common and interesting proof of the formal stability of an intuition recorded in the mind without conscious words—without, that is, any conceptual activity—is shown in the visual experience of a writer looking for a word he wants in order to express his meaning. He is sure that there is such a word; finally he hunts in his Roget and finds that it does not exist. He will have to express his meaning by a phrase; that is to say, the content of his imagination has failed to find its form in a word. It is a very common experience of the writer to discover that his content cannot be given form in words. He is obliged to sacrifice something, he is obliged almost always to sacrifice immediacy; that is to say, a strong and intense experience requires so many words for its expression that it becomes dilute. In that case, of course, the writer must attempt to convey it in action by inventing a situation, a scene between characters, which will convey to the reader the full impact of his intuition.

Since intuition is experience, the only way to fix and convey it is by art. Painters do it by a sketch, one of those vivid and summary sketches which, from a master's hand, are often more interesting and exciting to a professional eye than the finished work. Writers must do it by a similar work; a scene, a piece of dialogue.

Such a scene in my case was the one I have mentioned—at the railway station. It is not at the beginning of the book, but it was the first chapter completed, because it recorded for me an experience fundamental to the book's meaning. It is interesting to see how often novelists do, early in a book, give a scene which fixes some fundamental point of experience. In Conrad's *Lord Jim* the book starts right away with the scene where Jim, having been convicted by the court of cowardice and dereliction of duty, walks out a completely dishonoured man, an event that has happened thousands of times and happens every day. But Conrad in this first scene makes us feel what the disaster means for that young man at that time. He makes it real for us and fixes the intuition for himself in the sense that it passes beyond language, the merely descriptive word, to a fundamental and direct experience.

The scene need not always be dramatic. Dickens, at the beginning of *Bleak House*, gives us only the London fog. But that fog is the keynote of the whole. It gave Dickens back all the time, whenever he needed it, the sense of a dark, dirty and muddled world, of the confusion and despair of lost souls. This description is poetry by one of our greatest prose-poets, whose books, indeed, are conceived in the mood of the ballad. D. H. Lawrence, in another magnificent passage of prose poetry, gives us his whole intuition of life. This is on the second page of *The Rainbow*, his story of the Brangwen family. He writes of them:

They felt the rush of the sap in spring, they knew the wave which cannot halt, but every year throws forward the seed to begetting, and falling back, leaves the young-born on the earth. They knew the intercourse between heaven and earth, sunshine drawn into the breast and bowels, the rain sucked up in the daytime, nakedness that comes under the wind in autumn, showing the birds' nests no longer worth hiding. Their life and interrelations were such; feeling the pulse and body of the soil, that opened to their furrow for the grain, and became smooth and supple after their ploughing, and clung to their feet with a weight that pulled like desire, lying hard and unresponsive when the crops were to be shorn away. The young corn waved and was silken, and the lustre slid along the limbs of the men who saw it. They took the udder of the cows, the cows yielded milk and pulse against the hands of the men, the pulse of the blood of the teats of the cows beat into the pulse of the hands of the men. They mounted their horses, and held life between the grip of their knees, they harnessed their horses at the wagon, and, with hand on the bridle-rings, drew the heaving of the horses after their will.

Here we have the expression of Lawrence's whole intuition of life as lived finally at the level of fundamental passion and fundamental needs, of an order of life not reducible to logic or rational judgment.

Lawrence, in fact, like all the other significant writers of his generation, Aldous Huxley, Virginia

Woolf, Evelyn Waugh, is violently in revolt against the presuppositions of the generation before, of that school dominated by Galsworthy and Wells, for whom life was seen in terms of sociology, who assumed that what was wrong with society could be cured by legislation, who imagined that the injustices and tragedies of common life could be abolished by taking reasonable thought. Against this shallow idea, against also the shallow rationalism of the Lytton Strachey school, all these writers reacted powerfully in their various ways: Aldous Huxley in a defeatist mood saying that humanity was fundamentally vile and animal and its degradation not only incurable, but not worth curing; Virginia Woolf, with her creed that personal relations were all that mattered in life, emphasising the quality of the individual soul and its affections as against the statistical abstractions of the sociological school.

All were in revolt against a conceptual, a symbolic system, which had lost all meaning for them, which had become stale. This is shown vividly by Virginia Woolf's remark that Arnold Bennett had forgotten that man had a soul. This is not true of Bennett at his best. He had no religion and despised religion as he imagined it to be. He was, on the other hand, a sensitive and honourable person. He was therefore torn all his life between the crudest material values and his own critical distaste for what is crude and cheap. He did not so much forget the soul as deny it, at the same time as he was recording its movements. And I think this was why such a fine artist did not achieve his own greatness.

Bennett, although a far finer artist than Wells or Galsworthy, although inferior only to the great of his time, to Hardy, James and Conrad, expressed himself in the manner of his time. His prose is matter-of-fact, common-sensible, its mood is rationalistic, that of a man of the world. This is to say, only, that his books belonged to their period.

For although a writer's details from page to page may seem to have no special difference, the whole is always highly particular. To take an example from our own time, a page of Compton-Burnett's dialogue by itself is simply good prose; no doubt we might call it an old-fashioned style, in the symbols of the past; but the whole book, made of such prose, is completely original. That is to say, the form of a book, page by page, is not the book, the work of art. All these separate pages and chapters, like the movements of a symphony, do not have a complete significance until the whole work is known. They are, so to speak, partly in suspension, until at the end of the last movement, the last chapter, they suddenly fall into their place. This is only to say again that the separate forms do not possess their whole content until the work is complete. That's why I call the book a total symbol. It is both richer than its parts and actually different from them.

XXIII

REVOLUTION OF AN IDEOLOGY

IT was to this total symbol that Virginia Woolf reacted when she repudiated Bennett, and she so despised it that she also despised the man.

This scorn is typical of an original group in reaction against a superseded and exploded group. The Impressionists absolutely despised the traditionalists. They scorned not only their art but the men themselves. They talked about them as fools and contemptible time-servers, selling their aesthetic souls for cash. This was not merely the technical revolution of new genius against old academies, due to the prostitution or exhaustion of a symbolic system. It was also the revolution of an ideology. The Impressionist had a new idea of art as an impression of light and colour, the Lawrence-Woolf school had a new idea of life as fundamentally passionate, individual, irrational. They had, that is, a new *theme*.

We saw that what made that lunch-time conversation so significant to James was his theme, his idea of life, his valuation of the real. He thought of life as a tragedy for the fine, the good.

This theme, this view of life, therefore, directed James' intuition. But the theme was the product of a long course of reflection, of conceptual education. A child has intuition, but no theme. Everything is equally exciting to its imagination. But soon something happens to it which makes a special impression and if it acquires anywhere some explanation of the force and value of this impression, that explanation gives it an idea of the real which is rooted deeply in a vital experience.

So Tolstoy's religious training enforced his intense intuition of family love; it explained the value of love in the wörld, it gave his religious idea very deep roots in a personal experience of the real, finally it gave him his theme; that is to say, the theme had its tap-root in a first profound experience.

Though writers write from an idea (and, as I have said, everyone, not only writers, must have such an idea, merely in order to manage his life), ideas for living need not be based on any intuition. Many have as little relation to any fundamental experience as a time-table; and this is true of many writers who can't be said to have any themes at all. They have merely a notion for a book and the book has, therefore, no fundamental relation to reality and no real form.

But all great artists have a theme, an idea of life profoundly felt and founded in some personal and compelling experience. This theme then finds confirmation and development in new intuition. The development of the great writer is the development of his theme—the theme is part of him and has become the cast of his mind and character.

The yarn-spinner who works merely from happy thoughts, is continually looking for happy thoughts, for inspiration in events. He hunts for what is called material, but the great writer does not need material and the greater number of events are of merely passing interest to him. How much did Emily Brontë see of the world before she wrote *Wuthering Heights* or her poems? It is not certain that even the poems are founded in actual events. Her intuition of romantic and passionate love, her theme, was all she needed.

XXIV

REVELATION AND ART

THERE is a fascinating passage in the Countess Tolstoy's diary where she describes how Tolstoy, while meditating *Anna Karenina*, got the intuition for Anna's tragedy. It was not, as people suppose, from his being summoned to an inquest on a woman who had committed suicide on the railway line. The death and mutilation of this woman, whom he knew—who was the mistress of a friend—affected him deeply. And in the book he made Anna commit suicide on the railway. But it was not the suicide that gave him the important intuition, it did not belong to his theme.

For Tolstoy Providence, in giving to man the power of love and response to love, had provided him with the only necessary clue to the good life. Any form of society not based on love was evil and also unnatural. Nature, in short, as Tolstoy conceived it, was the will of God. The artificial life of society as opposed to that of the countryman or the peasant was especially corrupt.

In *Anna Karenina* he contrasted, therefore, what he considered the false and unnatural life of Anna and her friends with the natural and good life of Levin and Kitty. In this conception women and men have been allotted quite different natures by Providence. Woman's function was social, to be sister, wife, mother, nurse, the centre of family life, the builder and keeper of its sacred values. Anna's tragedy was that she left her husband and child for a lover. This destroyed not only her husband's happiness, but her lover's, and finally her life.

Tolstoy had his important intuition one morning when sitting in his dressing-gown which was embroidered in what was called Turkish work. Tolstoy noticing the work, was suddenly struck by its elaboration and delicacy, its patient precision. He thought some unknown woman did all that careful stitchery, and so he felt the profound difference of a woman's life, a woman's mind, and woman's world, from a man's. And this was directly illustrative of Tolstoy's theme, whereas the suicide did not belong to the theme, and therefore it suggested only an incident in the working-out, the conceptual planning of the work.

On the other hand, for Hardy, the suicide could have been the inspiration of a story or a whole book. For his theme was the injustice of life, the cruelty of blind fate destroying innocent and guilty alike. In *Tess of the d'Urbervilles* Angel Clare thinks of Tess as an innocent village girl, but Tess had been seduced before he met her. Tess, deeply in love with Clare, decides at last to confess to him before marriage. She writes him a note and pushes it under his bedroom door. Next morning he makes no reference to it, but she sees that it has disappeared and supposes that he has received it. In fact she puts down his silence therefore to magnanimity and is still more in love. By a mere accident it has slid under the carpet of the bedroom so that Clare has never seen it. So by this accident a confession that might have saved Tess's life fails of any effect. Tess's life is destroyed, not by any defect in her nature, not by any law of providence, but by mere bad luck.

For Hardy the ruling master of our tragedy was blind fate, for Tolstoy it was the nature of things, the laws of being. Anna represented womanhood. She broke God's law for womanhood, and was therefore not only the source of evil to others but was herself terribly punished.

Anna Karenina is a masterpiece of form, one of the finest ever written. Every fact, every character and incident, carries on the story, and enlarges the significance of the whole. It carried, therefore, with great power, Tolstoy's meaning which was also his message, his evangel, about the natural life, and about woman's place in the world according to her nature.

We are told that novelists must not preach. This is nonsense. All serious artists preach—they are perfectly convinced of the truth as they see it, and they write to communicate that truth.

The Kreutzer Sonata repeats Tolstoy's message with even greater force and prejudice. He tells us there that women are brought up only for the marriage market, taught from childhood to exploit their sex, that marriage itself is merely a sexual conspiracy or a sexual battle, and that from these causes arise all the evils of society. It is pure propaganda and we don't believe a word of it.

But because Tolstoy is a great artist, he has devised a form for his propaganda which makes it highly moving to us. He puts the message he wants to convey in the mouth of the protagonist, the wife-murderer, and he makes us feel that this man's obsession is completely true to his nature and to life. We say, 'A man like that no doubt believes all this nonsense, and that is why he killed his wife', or we may, more subtly, reflect, 'All this nonsense is the excuse of a jealous man to explain why he killed his wife'. The book gives us a fine picture of that everlasting type, the neurotic, frustrated or merely selfish and stupid person, who puts upon society the reproach of his own failure. So at the very time we are saying 'What nonsense', we are also saying, 'How true to the man—how true to the situation'.

The Kreutzer Sonata is completely successful as a work of art because, although it preaches, the message it is meant to give has been entirely assimilated into its form. The whole thing is an experience with the feeling appropriate to that form.

In the same way, even when we do not agree with Hardy's idea of life, we are struck by the fearful truth of his tale. In all the masters, with all their different ideas, we have over and over again that exciting sense of revelation, of new truth which only good art can bring us, and this truth is something we are looking for in the masters, something we expect from art.

If the themes of the masters are so different that they may, as with Hardy and Tolstoy, contradict each other, we have to ask, 'What do we mean by truth in art, and especially the novel?'

XXV

IDEA AND FORM

THE question of truth in art is an old one. It was always obvious that most writers were biased. And one school of novelists, the French school of the Goncourts, Flaubert, and finally Zola, set themselves deliberately to write novels that should be true to fact. They said, 'We shall have nothing to do with romance, with drama, we shall study life as it is, and write from life'. The consequence, for all four, was that they were accused of a libel on human nature and their countrymen. Flaubert was taken to court for *Madame Bovary*. He pleaded that he was interested only in art, he had no wish to attack anybody. This was, of course, untrue. Flaubert was intent on giving what he believed to be the truth about people, and especially the bourgeois, whom he detested. His prejudice was so violent that his last work, *Bouvard et Pécuchet*, a satire on two retired clerks, is unreadable. It is as boring as a tune on two notes. On the other hand, the attack on him was equally beside the point unless you believe in censorship. And Zola was even more violently abused for what was called his vicious distortion of the truth.

In *L'Assommoir* Zola sets his story in the Paris of the Second Empire. The plot turns on the drink traffic. His heroine Gervaise, a good, virtuous, decent working girl, marries Coupeau, a worker in zinc. They have a daughter, Nana. Gervaise starts a small laundry and does well. Then Coupeau has a fall, damages himself and takes to drink, and gradually ruins both himself and Gervaise. She is too gentle, too decent, or too weak to leave him or fight him. She ends on the streets and dies of exposure—Coupeau of delirium tremens at a hospital.

The book is a masterpiece, full of magnificent descriptions of working-class life in Paris at that time. And Zola studied every detail from life; the drink trade, the pubs, laundry work, the public laundries, a dozen crafts and the obscure courts where they were carried on. But the French accused him of giving a completely false picture of the Paris working class.

It is true that Zola probably exaggerated drunkenness among working men because he was writing about drink—a consequence of the book was the abolition by law of the kind of absinthe which destroyed Coupeau. From that time absinthe has been quite a different stuff. Drink was Zola's theme, and his plot is built upon it. Concentration upon drink as an evil among the working class was essential to him as a writer not only because he felt strongly about drink, but because he had to have a centre for his plot.

As Henry James writes to Hugh Walpole about his novel, *Mr Perrin and Mr Traill*,

> I don't quite recognise here the *centre of your subject*, that absolutely and indispensably fixed and constituted point from which one's ground must be surveyed and one's material wrought. If you can say it's (that centre) in Mr P.'s exasperated consciousness I can only reply that if it might be it yet isn't treated as such.

Without some unifying idea, it is impossible for a book to have a form. As Flaubert in *Madame Bovary* built his whole complex structure around Emma Bovary's romantic dream, so Zola built on the tragedy of Coupeau's drunkenness. Flaubert chose his characters, his background, to illuminate the dreams of a frustrated woman; he gives her a dull husband, and buries her in the boredom of a small country village, he ruins her through the moneylender who plays upon her love of finery.

He brings in the country Don Juan to make love to her at the agricultural prize-giving, and draws a provincial clerk whom she pursues in her turn at Rouen. We have, that is, the whole picture of a rural society, of its leading characters from the apothecary and the doctor to the farmers, tradespeople, the small squire, even a glimpse, in the famous ball, of its lords, constructed round Emma Bovary, to illustrate Flaubert's theme of the futility and vulgarity of middle-class existence. But without Emma Bovary's character and the story of her tragedy, it would have no form at all as a novel, it would not, so to speak, add up to a whole of meaning, an experience of Flaubert's world. *Madame Bovary* makes an unforgettable impact upon the reader. It is a permanent possession of his imagination. But it owes that memorable power even more to the formal unity of its plot than to the excellence of the writing, which is of course, seen as completed and achieved form, an aspect of that unity. The mood of the style is in the mood of the whole book. It affects even the choice of what should be in narrative, what in dialogue. But that unity is obtained by selection of facts, of characters, by special interpretation of events, which is partial and so far untrue. Country life is not necessarily a bore, country doctors are not necessarily fools, and their wives are often sensible, cheerful and even faithful. So Zola, in *L'Assommoir*, in order to achieve his form, was obliged to give a false impression of Paris working-class life as a whole. This is true of all novels. They must have an angle in order to have form and meaning, and this angle is usually even narrower, sweeps a narrower range of truth, than the writer's own angle, on account of the limitations of the craft itself. Zola's *Nana*, which succeeded *L'Assommoir*, giving us the life of the daughter as an actress and a demi-mondaine, deals throughout with that half-world of prostitution and the comedy theatre. Drink takes no place in it. It would simply complicate the plot, the form, without adding any significance to it. The truth of *Nana*, so strongly felt by the respectable bourgeois Zola, is a quite different truth from that of *L'Assommoir*, equally important in Zola's feeling. But as an artist, as novelist, he knew too much of his craft to attempt to combine them in one work.

He existed, like all of us, in his own particular world of fact and feeling, created in his imagination from childhood, and he could not write about any other. This picture gave him the valuation by which he selected from the confusion of the active scene what was significant to him. From what was significant, again, he selected that part which could be made significant in a novel, given the limitations of that art. He left out anything that could confuse the plot and therefore the reader.

For a reader must never be left in doubt about the meaning of a story. I mean, of course, the ideal reader; in the first place, the writer himself.

XXVI

LIMITATIONS OF FORM

So we have the position, a novel has to be a partial view of things. First, because all views are partial and personal, and secondly, because of the limitations of the form of thé novel, of which the first and most important is this: that the more comprehensive a novel in scope, in width of scene, the more it loses in power and significance. *Anna Karenina* has much more power than *War and Peace*, and *The Kreutzer Sonata* has more than *Anna Karenina*. The truth given by a novel is in close relation with the power of its expression. It is truth for feeling, it is truth about values. It is a personal truth. For Zola, drink was a fearful truth because it was a fearful evil, and to make light of it, to make it subordinate to any other issue in *L'Assommoir* would have been falsifying the truth of his feeling.

It is not valid to charge a writer with falsification because he emphasises one truth rather than another. As for saying that he does not give the whole, that is absurd because the whole truth cannot be known. It would have to include not only events which are happening all the time and changing the phenomenal world while I speak, but the valuation of events. The most important part of truth is what humanity is suffering, is feeling and thinking at any moment, and this cannot be known, as a totality, to any person. It is not known completely to the individuals themselves. For immediately life takes place in the subconscious, before it is known to reflection; and its sources, the active nature of being itself, are completely beyond the human imagination.

A novelist, therefore, can give only very partial truth in any one book, and that truth with an angle.

It is often said that the only truth a writer can give is a point of view, that the truth of a work of art is simply its coherence, its meaning as a work of art. The 'meaning' here is frequently given a pragmatic sense, as effect. A whole school of criticism, in the twenties, took this view. A work of art was to be judged by what it does to the reader, the observer. Its truth was merely in relation to that reader and could be a lie in any other relation. That is to say, it could be founded in the Nazi philosophy or in Marx, and if on that account it gave a Nazi or a Stalinite more satisfaction, say, than a masterpiece by a Tolstoy or a Hardy, it would be a greater and truer work.

This theory was in accord with the general fashion of thirty years ago; it was in reaction against the religiosity of the Victorians before and any belief in real values. It went with atheism, dadaism, Marxism, Freudianism and the rest. It is now old-fashioned and generally on the defensive. But it could find a lot of support still in the experience of writers and readers. For the first duty of a writer is to compose a form of meaning which shall be coherent to the reader, even if that reader be himself. And the meaning is addressed finally to the emotions, the sensibility. The writer must seize upon the sympathy of the reader for his characters, and as every professional knows, a major problem for the novelist is to maintain the emotional continuity of the work. To do this, even so masterly a technician as Jane Austen will break a rule. In the third chapter of *Pride and Prejudice* she writes about Mr Bingley that Mrs Bennet, being unable to draw from her husband any satisfactory description of the gentleman, was obliged to accept the second-hand intelligence of her neighbour, Lady Lucas. At the bottom of the page we read that Mrs Bennet said to her husband, 'If I can but see one of my daughters happily settled at Netherfield, I shall have nothing to wish for'.

This is something we know very well. Mrs Bennet, on the second page of the book has said already that she is thinking of marrying one of her daughters to Mr Bingley or his friend; that is to say, Jane Austen has repeated herself, a thing no novelist does if he can avoid it. A repetition at once brings before the reader's mind an anxious author trying to make a point, and authors ought not to be present in readers' minds.

Obviously Jane Austen repeats herself in order to show us that Mrs Bennet, having consulted Sir William and Lady Lucas about Mr Bingley, has now returned home. She cannot say so because the mere statement would break the emotional continuity, the mood of the book, consistently satiric from the beginning. Probably, too, as a technician she reflected or discovered that a remark by Mrs Bennet introducing any new matter would surprise and check the reader. The satiric vein has to continue unbroken in Mrs Bennet's words, but without attracting too much attention from the reader to their real purpose, that is, to get her home.

The transition, the handling of space in this case is so deft that probably only a professional would notice the technical device. Yet it is one in which Jane Austen has sacrificed a certain integrity in order to hold the reader in his mood, and that integrity of form is one of the things for which we chiefly value her, and, I imagine, she valued herself.

The reader thus carefully handled, is regarded, even in Jane Austen's day, a hundred years before any behaviourist theory of human conduct, as a mere reaction mass, a kind of emotional piano, on which the artist plays his little tune. This view seems true to our practice. How often are we told that to read we must put away all prejudice, relax, make ourselves completely receptive, await reactions.

This attitude of the writer towards his readers is founded not on any *a priori* theory but on experience. Every writer as reader and critic of his own work is aware of emotional continuity as a prime technical demand of his craft. And this gives at once a very strong support to the behaviourist theory of art— that art has nothing to do with truth or the representation of any objective real. It is intended to produce certain psychological reactions in a passive mind.

All the same, I think it completely false. In the first place, we do, as readers, notice a difference between truth of art and truth of revelation. We can enjoy a masterpiece of form without in the least accepting it as true. Our meaning when we say, 'That's good', is quite different from the sense of revelation with which we say, 'That's true'. We accept *The Kreutzer Sonata* as a masterpiece of form, but we don't accept its meaning as a general truth. And this sense of revelation certainly appears to be the same as that with which we intuit the real.

XXVII

CREATIVITY AND THE SUBCONSCIOUS

THIS suggests a completely new approach to the question: what happens in reading?

In the first place, the reader is receptive only in a special sense. Actually, what a reader has in front of him is simply a collection of marks on paper, inert and meaningless in themselves. They are incapable on their own account of giving him anything. Reading is a creative art, subject to the same rules, the same limitations as the imaginative process by which any observer of the arts turns a mere lump of stone, colours scattered on a canvas, noise, things completely meaningless in themselves, into a formal impression. The meaning received is created by the imagination from the symbols, and that imagination must first be educated—as the artist himself was educated—in the use and meaning of a symbolic system. The reader may believe that he is completely receptive and uncritical, he may and should attempt to expose himself to an experience without prejudice, but in fact he is performing a highly active and complex creative act. The reason he does not notice it is because most of it takes place in the subconscious.

Only small children, when they first learn to read, are obliged to examine each word by itself and to reflect on its meaning. Even with small children the reaction soon becomes automatic; in a very short time they cease to consider the words and are entirely preoccupied with their effect.

In the second place, though the conscious mind does recognise certain subtleties of style, certain felicities of reference to what we might call scholarly details—for instance, a side-glance by James Joyce at Aquinas—such intellectual distinctions either appeal also to the sensibility, and work in with the general emotional meaning, the orchestra as a whole, or they check the appreciation of that meaning, and so fail to cohere in the form. They are entirely superfluous and harmful, or they are, for nine-tenths of their effect, operative in the subconscious with the rest of the work. The essence of that work for the reader is that there should be no check to his emotional satisfaction, that the meaning of words and phrases should be directly apprehended, that the continuity of the activity building the total experience in the memory should proceed without check for inquiry.

Jane Austen's intuition of the character of a reader is perfectly sound. She understood that the writer is dealing in the reader with a subconscious process in which the logic is that of emotional association. She understood that the emotional continuity in a book was all-important.

I suppose that everyone will accept this fact in the case of a symphony which has no factual or conceptual meanings. But it is just as true of a novel, which is also art in line, that is, it is not apprehended simultaneously in all its elements like a picture, it builds in the memory, and it is not complete until all has been read, until it becomes a total symbol, a total meaning. Yet at once, when this total effect has been felt, not only do all the details assume a new and final relation to the whole, but we are aware of the judgments which assessed them at the time of reading.

That is to say, critical reflection has been made, without in the least interrupting the flow of what has seemed like passive experience. But what is interesting to notice is that even when the reader, checked by some inconsistency, stops to examine it, he is usually obliged to re-read the passage, in a conscious critical spirit, in order to find out exactly what has broken the spell. This seems to mean that, though the critical power has asserted itself, it has done so at first through the sympathetic feelings engaged in pure enjoyment of the work of art as created for them by the subconscious. The reader feels a check in what we have called the emotional continuity of his experience. This check is felt even if the failure is not at all in the continuity of feeling but merely in some matter of fact, if the writer has made roses bloom in April or sent his hero hunting in June, or merely forgotten the colour of his heroine's eyes. For though the facts of a book have no importance except as supporting the theme, yet, as the breaking of an armature may bring down the finest of models, so the dislocation of an argument may destroy the form of a chapter.

By armature here I mean the factual frame as designed for that book; and by its dislocation I *don't* mean the kind of fantastic coincidence or improbability which we find, for instance, in Dickens. Dickens' plots are perfectly to his purpose. He is a romantic prose poet dealing in melodrama. What would pull us up in Dickens would be a turn from Jane Austen or Richardson.

By dislocation I mean something incongruous to the author and the book in hand. And the first effect of such incongruity is merely a moment of uneasiness and a break in the dream. One wakes up as it were and says, 'Hullo, what's this? What's wrong?' Then one re-reads the passage in this new vein of curiosity, of critical inquiry, and discovers the flaw.

For such a check in the work of a master, look at the last sentence of chapter III, book III of *Madame Bovary*. We are in the middle of Emma Bovary's love affair with Léon the clerk at Rouen. Her excuse for visiting Rouen is to prepare a power of attorney with the lawyer, on which Léon as lawyer's clerk is to give his advice.

We have then a whole chapter of their romantic love affair. They part, and Léon is left with his intoxicated memories of the day. Then suddenly we have the passage: 'But why', he asks himself afterwards while he goes home alone through the streets, 'is she so keen to get this power of attorney?' And then the next chapter returns immediately to the clerk's romantic obsession. This sentence about the power of attorney checks the reader at once. There is no reason on earth why the clerk should think at that moment about the power of attorney. It is quite out of key with his mood. He is not given any trace of cynicism to explain it.

Of course in actual life any young man, even without being a cynic, would make such a remark. Actual young men may be as scatter-brained as you please. But Léon is not an actual young man. He is a motif in a work of art and that motif, especially at this moment, is one of romantic passion. To make him break off his mood to talk about powers of attorney is as though Verdi should permit his *prima donna* in the midst of her aria to stop and blow her nose. What's more, the reader being checked by this passage, and asking himself why Flaubert should do such a thing, at once sees a reason. It seemed to him necessary to give, at this point, a reminder of the plot.

There you have the conceptual preoccupation of the writer suddenly obtruded into the emotional continuity of his theme at the point where the emotion was especially strong and the continuity extremely important.

Flaubert is a master of symphonic form, and I cannot remember any similar check in the whole of *Madame Bovary*. It is worth noting that its cause is preoccupation with the plot. To keep the reader in touch with the details of a plot is always a problem for a writer. They have to be conveyed within the texture of feeling, and there is always a temptation to distort psychology in order to bring them in at the right place.

XXVIII

MIND AND EDUCATION

So while the reader seems to himself to be submitting passively to the complex experience offered to him by a book or a piece of music, he is actually extremely active on three or four different levels. His subconscious is creating or reconstructing from the symbols before him the whole emotional content of the work; his reflective judgment is all the time recording flaws of expression, failures of emphasis, loose joints and weak transitions; and some part of that judgment operating at the level of what seems like the pure receptivity, is ready at once to notice an error of fact, even when that error does not destroy the continuity of the emotional experience.

In this highly complex process, not only the creative imagination, the sympathies, the critical taste, are brought into play, but also knowledge of all kinds, of fact as well as art, of actuality as well as books. Conceptual knowledge, even when it has not sunk into the subconscious, is valuable to the reader as to all other creative artists; it enables him actually to compose for himself a richer expression, a deeper, more complex experience. Let us take for example a simple book like *Northanger Abbey*. I lent that once to a schoolboy of thirteen staying with us for the holidays in a seaside villa. The day was wet and he had nothing to do. He was by no means a reader, but boredom drove him to read *Northanger Abbey* and he enjoyed it so much that he asked me if Austen had written anything else. What he had enjoyed, apparently, was Catherine's quality as a girl, Thorpe's swagger and the scene at Northanger Abbey where Catherine imagines horrid mysteries.

All of us can enjoy the book at this level, but how much richer is an appreciation of it as part of Jane Austen's development and self-revelation; as a criticism of the horror school and a reaction against it; as a masterpiece of the completely mature and civilised culture of the eighteenth century, a culture at the top of its wave, translucent throughout, but just about to tumble into roaring confusion.

Everything we know about Jane Austen, about social history, about literature and literary fashion, about religion, about the position of women in her time, adds to our power of enjoyment. For we not only feel in the subconscious; we judge, we reason, we carry out quite elaborate logical inquiries without knowing it.

The mind, in short, by education, has acquired a complex formal character which has all the spontaneity of primitive emotional make-up. The feelings are charged with ideas and the ideas with feeling, and reflection can proceed without conscious thought.

How often the artists, card-players, mathematicians, and scientists have told you that when you are stumped for the answer to a problem, you should simply forget it, or better, sleep on it. They relate how they have waked in the small hours with the solution in their minds. And this is not surprising to anyone who knows the world of symbols and the logic of associations, the dream world in which we spend so much of our lives, not only when we are asleep. I suspect that the inspirations of artist and scientist both arise from the logic of the subconscious, carried on by a method far more rapid and effective than that of conceptual logic, by short-cuts of pure association. Subconscious logic is the means without which no novelist should write dialogue. It would be impossible for him at every change of speaker to stop and ask 'What sort of a character is this, how would he feel at this point, and how should he speak?' He becomes by intuition that character for that moment. It is the same familiar sympathetic action by which we enter into a friend's feelings and *know* his mood.

This, of course, is how Dostoevsky was led into the dilemma of Ivan's argument in 'Pro and Contra'. For that moment he *was* Ivan Karamazov and as Ivan he argued far too well for his plot. He broke through his own concept of what the plot was to be and made for himself a new discovery of Ivan's force of mind and truth.

I suppose every writer has had experience of this subconscious working. When I was in New York in 1953 an American friend, Elizabeth Lawrence of Harper's, took me round Manhattan Island in a steamer. It was late October, the deck wasn't crowded, and presently a woman came to an empty seat on the other side. For some reason this woman caught my eye, and I said to my friend, quite unexpectedly to myself, 'I could write about that woman'. She asked me why, and I said I didn't know, but we both looked at her with some interest. She was, I suppose, in her middle thirties, a spinster, dressed in a neat but rather shabby coat and skirt and what you might call a useful hat. She was neither plain nor pretty, and I noticed that her forehead was very deeply wrinkled. She hadn't a particularly easy life, but she had come to enjoy herself on the steamer, and was listening with amused attention to the spieler, an Irish American, who was putting on a tremendous brogue. I asked Elizabeth Lawrence, 'Who do you suppose she is, and where does she come from?' Elizabeth thought she might be a school-teacher from the Middle West making her first trip to New York, 'Or perhaps she is a daughter at home looking after a sick mother, and escaped for the day'.

Often when I see someone or something I feel I could write about, I make a note, but actually I forgot all about this woman. Some weeks later at San Francisco, I woke up at 3 o'clock in the morning with so acute a sense of a story that I turned on the light and wrote two or three key pages of talk and description. I had an engagement for the next day but it fell through, and while I was wondering what to do with myself I remembered this sketch. I turned it up, I found it again interesting, and I worked at it all day. By evening I had a complete draft, all but the polish.

XXIX

LOGIC AND THE SUBCONSCIOUS

THE story was about a man in his forties who had lost his wife. He had a small daughter of ten and he decided he ought to marry again, if only for her sake. His marriage had been, as he supposed, successful. But it had its disagree-ments. He was no longer romantic about love. He said to himself, I'll use my common sense and choose a thoroughly useful, good-tempered person as house-keeper for myself and step-mother for my daughter. Just at this time he met a girl whom he had known as a child at the seaside. He had been very fond of her, they had been good comrades, and he introduced himself again, but the girl was with friends and even while he was talking to her he realised that she was still a good comrade, but the comrade was now a woman—she wasn't at all suitable to be his wife. However, she was delighted to meet him and she begged him to go and see her mother, who was still living.

He duly visited the mother and met the second daughter, who had been the beauty of the family, rather spoilt. She was now married, a spoilt wife and a poor lily. But while he was dining he noticed a little woman of about thirty, very quiet and plain, who was taking care of all the arrangements. He hadn't been introduced to her, but presently the mother called her Francie and he remembered that there had been a third girl in the seaside party, a child of six or seven, at the grubbiest stage of child-hood, who was always being scolded or sent on messages. He realised that this quiet and reserved woman had been this child, and he thought suddenly, 'Why shouldn't she suit me—she is well broken-in to domestic life, she won't expect a great deal in marriage, she will probably be rather pleased and grateful to get a husband at all'.

So he approached the girl and she accepted him. They were married. Since, however, he was a decent fellow, he thought it unfair to marry a girl of thirty and not give her a baby if she wanted one—and in fact she had a couple of children. But both the spoilt sister and the mother were always sending for her; in any family crisis they telephoned for Francie to come and cook the dinner, or fetch the children from school. At last, the doctor intervened with the man and said, 'This can't go on, your wife is not very strong, she is nursing a second baby in two years, she is very busy in your own house, she mustn't do all this extra work, and you must stop it'. But when he tried to stop it Francie was terribly upset and asked him what he wanted her to do. If she didn't solve her mother's domestic problems, the mother would certainly not be able to keep a maid and would have to live with them. As for the poor lily, she was quite unfit to look after her own children and if Francie didn't go to help they would suffer.

So at the end of the story he is sitting in the car on a wet night, outside his mother-in-law's house, waiting to take his wife home. She has been summoned to cook a dinner and look after the guests. She runs out to him and he starts the engine, but she has come out only to say that she has got to go back for another ten minutes or so because someone has lost an umbrella.

He is left in desperation because he has fallen in love with this girl—he is in love for the first time in his life and yet he sees that the very things for which he loves her, her unselfishness, her strength of affection, are breaking her health, and may take her from him.

The short story needed, like all short stories, a great deal of polishing, and, some days later I was working on it, when I put my pencil for the third time through the word 'wrinkles'—that is to say I had repeated for the third time that Francie had a deeply wrinkled forehead. And as I did so that girl on the Manhattan boat jumped into my consciousness, and I realised where the story had come from. I don't mean to say that all this story as written had been in that scribbled note. It had only the essential fact that a man making a sensible second marriage for convenience, fell in love for the first time and found that this great happiness also brought him great anxiety and distress. His life was at once enormously enriched and much more troubled.

I invented everything else in the working out. But the essentials were straight from the subconscious where they had formed themselves round an intuition, which had itself never emerged into conscious statement. I did not attach any ideas of character or situation to that girl on the boat. I did not get so far as to examine my own interest in her appearance. But obviously my intuition was itself conditioned by an attitude to life, otherwise I should not have had the immediate impression that I could write about her. This intuition, belonging to a view of life, and therefore a theme, proceeded to construct in my mind while asleep, or possibly to assemble from odds and ends of observation and reflection already there, a story with the necessary central characters and development.

This construction was logical in the sense that it developed a story according to laws of psychology as they were assumed by the theme—the story was a fable illuminating a truth of reality. And so far it was a new thing. The subconscious created a new thing which was yet a logical development of what was already known to it, so well known that it had become subconscious. Now I can suggest that when the reader feels that shock of revelation, which is also recognition, when he says 'But that is true', he is undergoing the same process in his own subconscious. The writer has created for him characters and situations that he accepts as true because they accord with his experience. Suddenly the character does or says something that is new and unexpected to the reader, but the logic of his subconscious, furnished already with certain truths about character, and especially this character, declares at once 'But of course, that is how he would feel, he would speak'. Just as an author's imagined character, as Dostoevsky's Ivan, can give him a new intuition about a real world, so characters in a book can by sympathy reveal new truth to a reader.

Without this power of sympathy, there is no revelation. Sympathy is essential to the reader and writer. But by sympathy the reader can obtain from the created world of art a knowledge of truth, of the real world, with exactly the same sense of illumination as if he had discovered it by force of intuition. So the reader's process of creative discovery follows the same course as the writer's, from vivid childish intuition of the real, through education, back to the fresh intuition of a more complex reality, which includes not only the isolated facts seen by the child but the relation of these facts in his own private world of meaning. And the whole takes place within a developed character as personality.

The reader, as child, knows directly affection, anger, indifference, something of goodness and badness in people, and draws certain conclusions from them. But his realm of grasp is small. He has no idea of the larger social relations, of development, of change, or political and religious pressure. He must acquire these gradually in growing up, in education both by events and books: so that as educated man, he knows everything in a setting of relations, often extremely complex. He has comprehensive ideas about morals as well as the original intuition simply of good and bad acts revealed entirely in the narrow light of a child's personal feelings. And when, in reading, he says to himself 'That is true', his sense of discovery is founded in a knowledge that has given him all the premisses of his deduction. But the deduction is largely in the subconscious. It is reached by a logic of association, not by the reader's conscious analysis, and he is again in the position of the child whose direct intuition is spontaneous and without reflection.

xxx

MORAL JUDGMENT

THE important point here is that this secondary intuition has overcome the limitations of the concept, by passing beyond it into a realm of free association. No doubt the very weakness of the symbol in depending merely upon associations, its very lack of conceptual precision, contributes to this effect. But a still more effective cause in the liberation of the reader from the tyranny of the concept is that the whole process, not only of his feeling, but his reasoning, has become subconscious and automatic.

This does not mean that the reader has become a reaction-mass. We saw that the theory based on this conception in the nineteen-twenties is rightly disregarded nowadays. It has the prime defect that it does not explain to a reader his own experience, it does not explain his sense of revelation when he reads a truth. It does not explain why this sense is quite different from his approval of a stroke of mere technical brilliance. It does not explain the claim of

134

all art to deal with reality. When I say, therefore, that reading in an educated man has become largely sub-conscious, an automatic process, I am emphasising merely a development similar to that of the slow acquisition of skill by which a painter learns to handle his brush or a pianist to use his fingers. The hands of a pianist, by training, achieve an automatism which demands no thought from him while he plays, but this means only that they have become so perfect an instrument for his expression that he can give all his mind to the interpretation of the music.

Although reading may become almost completely automatic, the reasoning mind, the conceptual judgment, is always present to intervene, to criticise, and to record its critical judgment, which, at the end of the book reflects upon the whole experience and sums up its whole value.

But this judgment is now an integrated part of the intuitive character. It would be impossible for the reader to separate his emotional response from the critical judgment which is its form; which has taken so large a part in the development of his sensibility. We have, therefore, a picture of exploration of a realised scene, by the formed character of readers who have largely escaped from the limitations of the concept, and it is by intuition no different from that of a child's that they know the world.

Of course moral sensibility has exactly the same history of development, from the first intuitions of moral feelings and moral action through the education by history, by experience, by religious instruction, to something like a systematic judgment, which is at once rational and emotional. Though this is not our subject at the moment, it cannot be left out in considering the novel, as we shall see later on; and I'm not sure if it is not an ingredient, in every aesthetic judgment, of all the arts. We certainly distinguish between aesthetic and moral judgment; we say, for instance, of *The Kreutzer Sonata*, 'It is brilliant work, but morally it is all wrong, I don't believe a word of it'. But I suspect that our aesthetic judgment is still charged with a certain sensibility which we must call moral. We are struck, for instance, by a certain dignity and distinction in the handling of the story. With all its violence it has nothing exaggerated, nothing of what we call a false note, and these are moral attributes derived from a moral taste. If we compare *The Kreutzer Sonata* with some other tale of violence, let us say, *No Orchids for Miss Blandish*, we see at once a difference that is not purely aesthetic. You can say, if you like, that it resides in the mind of the writer, in his attitude towards violence, towards the whole story; but that is simply to say that moral sensibility is part of his genius. One cannot, in fact, split up the personality of a man—the sensible character of his being—into the aesthetic and the moral.

It is the whole man, the total sensibility that intuits the world. That world is a world of ordered meaning, of coherent value as given by art.

This is why the reader is often aware of learning more about the world from a book than he gets from actual experience, not only because in the book he is prepared to find significance in events that mean nothing in life, but because those events in the book are related to each other in a coherent valuation which sets them in ordered relation of importance, and this can reveal to him in what had seemed the mere confusion of his daily affairs new orders of meaning.

To get this coherence of meaning as a set of ordered values in a work of art, the writer selects his facts. He arranges their order to suit his own conception of values, his own theme, and these themes, as we saw in the case of Hardy and Tolstoy may be entirely different; they may even contradict each other. How can we say that both are true? How is it that we feel the truth of both authors? How can we feel that both of them are true to some reality objective to themselves?

The truth we find in both is truth in a context: in *Anna Karenina* truth both of character and of moral development. We say, given those characters, so they might act and suffer not only in the book but in reality. We may not agree with Tolstoy's philosophy, but that does not affect the force of our experience in the book any more than it would affect the force of our reaction when we read the lives of men with a different religion.

In the same way we accept the truth of Hardy, we

realise the force of his fundamental intuition, that much of fate is blind, that injustice is a permanent and inescapable element in reality, and we follow with sympathy the moral consequences for those who suffer it.

I have dealt here chiefly with writers because there the judgment of truth most obviously applies. It is, of course, applied often enough in architecture, painting and music, but without the same confidence. Obviously, in fact, the propriety of such judgments turns on the validity of Keats' statement, that 'beauty is truth, truth beauty'.

Has this statement any basis? I suggest, with all diffidence, that it does mean something of importance; that when we recognise beauty in any ordered form of art, we are actually discovering new formal relations in a reality which is permanent and objective to ourselves, which is part of that real that includes both human nature and its reactions to colour, line, mass and sound, and the material consistencies which maintain them. That is, we are recognising aesthetic meaning in the character of the universe, and this aesthetic order of meaning gives us the same sense of belonging to a rational and spiritual whole of character as does the moral truth of a Dante or Tolstoy.

When the Impressionists devised their new technique to express and reveal their new intuition, they gave us a revelation of a beauty no one had seen before. But it had always been potential in the actual nature of the world of colour, light, paint and human sensibilities. They revealed a truth as a scientist reveals a new element. Such an element is true in the deepest sense. It is part of the universal order of things.

But the school of David and Ingres rejected by the Impressionists was equally valid. How can we have two different truths within the same order, the same context?

Canaletto and Turner both painted the Grand Canal, and their pictures are completely different. Both are sincere expressions of the artist's realisation, and both are true to the facts, and to a real of feeling. When I say they are true to the facts, I mean they represent material fact in such a way that it can be identified. But this is not important except in so far as an aesthetic value belongs to the recognition of the fact. The Dome of the *Salute* for instance, as symbol, has all sorts of values—historical, religious, architectural—and none of these can be excluded from the meaning of the picture. The associations belonging to any symbol immediately gather about it in any context, so that it is impossible, for instance, in looking at that family picture I mentioned, to exclude the emotions excited by my aunt's hat, or the moral associations belonging to the idea of a late Victorian interior.

The facts in Turner and Canaletto are in the picture as values. If they were wrongly stated, they would spoil our appreciation or actually confuse us, so that we should fail to comprehend the picture as a meaning. Truth to the material fact is, therefore, a value in the whole construction of values, but a minor one.

What is important is the value given to the facts, and this is true in both these pictures, so completely different. What I mean is that it is valid for both Turner and Canaletto to find and express such meanings, so that we, seeing both pictures, can say of both, 'But that's true', meaning not only that's what Venice was to Canaletto and Turner, but that's what it could mean to us. We do not see it with Canaletto's or Turner's eyes, but we are transported into a context of feeling new to us, as, in first reading Homer, we enter into a primitive world and recognise its truth. We feel as if we have had a new experience. Both Turner's and Canaletto's Grand Canals are true expressions and true revelations of the real both in fact and feeling.

Of course, both could have been false to fact and feeling. They could have mis-stated the facts and expressed feeling completely untrue to the intuition, unrelated to any intuition of the scene. There are plenty of pictures of the Grand Canal which express nothing but a wish to paint the scene. They convey nothing but this wish, and give nothing of the real as value. They add nothing to one's knowledge or the reach of one's imagination. They do not teach us to see a new beauty or to rediscover an old one.

A Turner or Canaletto recreated in the imagination of an observer is unique for that observer. I said how my family picture became, in forty years, a different picture, or rather acquired new associations which immensely enriched it. That picture would have different associations for any observer. No two people can possibly see the same picture in the same way, or read the same book. In short, there are as many personal meanings in a work of art as there are persons to appreciate, and each can find there his own truth. The truth of a work of art is in its value both of fact and feeling. But feelings are indivisible and not subject to any exact analysis. And just as in our lives, among all the people we have known who have been our friends, there are not two alike, even in similar qualities of affection or generosity, wisdom or wit, and yet we can delight in each, in his special quality, so there are an infinite variety of such worlds. Infinity is a big word to use, especially in the context of an argument, emphasising the limited nature of reality. This limitation is very present to the artist. The painter has only his three primary colours, the composer his very short range of audible sound and the writer deals essentially with the very few elementary passions. The whole of plastic, literary and musical art has been built with these fundamental materials. Their infinite variety is not due to any extension of the spectrum or the gamut or to any change in fundamental human feeling but to a continuous expansion and enrichment of human sensibility.

141

That too, of course, is limited by human nature; but the emotions are subject to neither analysis, division or measurement. So they can exist in an endless variety of qualities and intensities, both for the artist who expresses them and for those who receive his meaning, in an infinity of creation like that of history which never repeats itself, and for ever produces novel and unexpected events with the same constants of human and material nature. That is to say, history, and the arts which are so closely woven into the fabric of historical process, display an infinite variety and novelty of actual consequences.

That's why not only Canaletto and Turner can be equally true but there are still possible any number of true pictures of the Grand Canal. Alternatively, there are possible any number of new false ones.

It can be objected that listeners to a symphony do not say, 'That is true', and in architecture, they use the word only about details of construction. So they speak of Wren's outer walls at St Paul's as false, but of the whole cathedral they use such words as grand, fine, beautiful, dignified.

The arts differ in the nature of their truth and its presentation. One does not go to a symphony for the same kind of experience as arises from a novel. Painters indeed tell you that no picture should have any literary reference—their art must concern itself only with colour and line. But this dogma belongs with the revolutionary slogans of fifty years ago when

Victorian art was attacked. It is, of course, based on a fallacy, that any art can be shut up in a compartment and secluded from all others. It is a form of the 'art for art's sake' cry invented in the eighteen-eighties in an attack on the moralistic critics of that day. As I said, the Dome of the *Salute* in a Canaletto, my aunt's hat in my family picture both carry moral and religious implications which therefore enter into the meaning of their respective pictures. Every art is enriched by meanings from the rest. Deliberately to exclude such meanings, as in some forms of abstract painting and sculpture, is simply to impoverish that art. It becomes a minor aesthetic; the art of teacups and wall-paper.

All the great masters of painting and sculpture without exception refer to a general knowledge of literature, history and aesthetics which belongs to every observer by dint of his education. This is true as much of Picasso and Henry Moore as Raphael, Titian or Michelangelo.

But there is this all-important truth in the distinction between the arts. Painters, sculptors, architects and composers do not intuit a moral real, or attempt to express it. They are dealing entirely with sensuous reality in colour, sound and form, and their works are aimed in the first place only at a sensuous reaction. This does not exclude a moral effect. There is certainly a connection between purely sensuous reality and emotional consequences. It is not pure fantasy to say that the colour red is like the sound of a trumpet, meaning that it inspirits and encourages. Size, and especially height, in a building, quite apart from symbolic associations, gives certain feelings of respect and awe, or, on the contrary, provokes defiance. To speak of the refinement of Rheims or certain modern buildings such as the Lever Building in New York, is not merely a metaphor, any more than it is for a mathematician to speak of the beauty of a proof. Economy of means, clarity of statement, concentration of function, and subtlety of detail all imply moral as well as aesthetic intuition.

A friend of mine tells me that a Beethoven symphony can solve for him a problem of conduct. I've no doubt that it does so simply by giving him a sense of the tragedy and the greatness of human destiny, which makes his personal anxieties seem small, which throws them into a new proportion.

But music, painting, sculpture do not take a moral problem as their theme and meaning; whereas all the written arts, except the purely factual, do nothing else. And the factual, however much they stick to facts, even the report of a wedding or a funeral, have no interest for us except in so far as they support or illustrate some moral value. So that when we speak of the novelist and poet's revelation of truth we mean that it is essentially moral, that it asserts a moral meaning in the real, and that we can check the meaning by reference to our knowledge of that real. For example, Dickens' indignant picture of a London waif in *Dombey and Son* made his readers say,

'That's how the poor wretch would feel, would react', and gave them an indignation that was now also discovered to them as belonging to their own general feeling of what was right and wrong. They had no doubt that their indignation was not merely the consequence of Dickens' skill in working up their feelings, but that it was justified in the actual world. It belonged to their moral conviction about that world even if they had not noticed it before.

The writer, then, creates for us a whole of meaning which is essentially moral. It is particular to himself in its angle and intensity, but we judge the truth of his work by its revelation of a moral real. Dickens' emphasis and art are particular to himself, but he reveals a general truth. Flaubert's angle towards bourgeois life is particular and we need not accept it, but we accept the tragedy of *Madame Bovary* as a powerful exposition of a moral truth, that such a woman behaving in such a way ought to suffer that fate.

In the actual world, of course, Madame Bovary might easily have escaped her fate. She could have found a rich lover and eloped with him, or inherited a fortune and paid her debts. In short, she could have been saved by a stroke of luck. But for Flaubert, luck was not important in the meaning he gave to the world, and so he disregarded it when he created for us a fable to illuminate a moral reality which, for him, underlay the actual world. We don't, in fact, admit the idea of luck in our sense of right and wrong, of truth and fantasy. We know it in the actual world, but we do not let it affect our moral judgment. We don't say that a man is good because he is lucky. We should not have excused Madame Bovary for ruining her faithful husband and neglecting her child even though she had eloped successfully with a lover and won a prize in a lottery. The form of *Madame Bovary* is, therefore, Flaubert's moral idea imposed upon the chaos of the actual world, and it is this which gives the events of the actual world meaning for us and this meaning as a moral judgment is rational and true.

XXXI

GOOD AND EVIL

ART has its immense power for good and evil because it deals always with fundamental passions and reactions common to all humanity. Even in its simplest forms, a single phrase of music, a colour pattern, it can give a shock of pleasure which makes life valuable. For that enjoyment has no relation with appetite or self-satisfaction. It is something freely given, a good, a grace, belonging simply to existence, to reality itself. For that minute, the meaning of existence is this special pleasure, the emotion of beauty.

In its more complex forms it carries man permanently out of the squalor and boredom of material needs and appetites, out of a mechanical existence into a world of achievement where he becomes by imagination a hero or a saint. For, as enjoyer, as observer or reader, he creates his own world and is master of it—just as the poor factory girl going to the films becomes for that afternoon a triumphant beauty or a princess, and discovers by that experience something of love and distinction. This, of course, may be the ruin as well as the joy of the girl, according to her idea of life, her moral judgment, her character. Her whole aim is to achieve herself and that achievement is always ideal and imaginative. Poetry, legends, invented and contrived by romantic students and their professors to swell out the fantastic cult of some Ruritania, can give frustrated clerks or labourers some dignity of self-respect. It can also turn them into murderers capable of any cruelty. But in each case they are achieving a dream. No one has ever pursued material gain for its own sake; even the miser, so far as he is not mad, values his money only as his achievement, his power, his dignity, or the defence of his dream. This is the meaning, the real meaning of his life.

Art is creation of meanings for the senses and the sensibility, the whole man. As the architect makes his new forms, for our new feeling, from the old material elements, within the limitation of weight and tension, so the composer organises his symphony and the novelist his tale. All transport us from the mechanical and blind existence of material causation into the world of personal value, of personal achievement, of meaning for action. They are not in the first place concerned with action or the practical reason. They build the dream for the imagination. But it is because all men live in such dreams and realise themselves in their dreams that art affects conduct. Hitler gave his frustrated and bewildered middle class the dream of glory, of racial superiority, of heroic destiny. They achieved themselves in a dream of superhuman will, of revenge and conquest, which they desired to realise in the actual world. That is to say, they would create a world to express their dream just as every artist creates his work of art. Unluckily for them, the dream was not realisable in actual form, it had taken no account of that reality which stands over against all dreams, all the creations of art, as a permanent character of nature, both in men and things. Hitler's was the kind of dream which fills the asylums with emperors and gods, men who have created for themselves impossible worlds.

Hitler, with his art of the demagogue, did immense evil. But great preachers, with a similar rhetoric, have done immense good. They have opened to millions power of achievement in an ideal world that does not conflict with the realities of existence. They have given a meaning to life which can make it a glory and a joy to live, even for the poorest, the most unlucky and frustrated, but which is true, which does not conflict with the real.

All the arts can give this meaning to life. We know that for Beethoven, stone deaf and deeply embittered, every moment of existence was precious for achievement. But each art has its special sphere of effect; music and poetry more sensuous, philosophy or mathematics more imaginative.

All the written and spoken arts, since they deal with an historical actuality, are bound to give meaning to human action which is always part, and commonly the greater part, of their theme. Music, sculpture, architecture, painting, are not concerned with events. That is why they are sometimes called the pure arts. They offer a purely sensuous and emotional whole of experience. They do not appeal to the practical or critical judgment except in so far as it is concerned with technical achievement. They excite, they stimulate, they give that intuition of the world of values which may and often has direct effect on moral judgment and moral action, but they do not deal with that judgment and that action, as a subject matter. For a writer, what men think and do is quite as important as what they are. A novelist creates a world of action and therefore he has to deal with motive, with morality. All novels are concerned from first to last with morality.

This is true even of Laclos and his *Liaisons Dangereuses* or, for a modern example, *No Orchids for Miss Blandish*. Both picture vice and cruelty, and depend for effect on shock. But the shock is a moral shock. Upon a person without any moral reactions or judgment they would have no effect. That is to say, the novelist addresses his meaning finally to the moral judgment. His whole apparatus of characters, plot, and description is designed to give knowledge of a world, his world, in which men, as he understands them, work out their destiny as moral beings. It is the same thing for Aeschylus or Dickens.

We judge the value of the work finally by its revelation of a moral real. The power and quality of the artist's craft is in the force and authority of his revelation. Proust's elaborate and subtle analysis of motive, his wonderful portraits, his brilliant scene-painting would be nothing to us without his moral preoccupation which appears in every line. If you don't believe this, examine your reaction while you read. You will find that all the time, at the very centre of your preoccupation, a moral judgment is at work, inquiring, comparing, discovering.

We are only not always aware of this fact because it is elementary and habitual in all reading. It is the form that gives unity to the experience.

XXXII

THE MORAL CONSTANT

WE accept for this experience the author's factual world, his background, as comparatively unimportant. Thus, we read the Bible narrative of Abraham, Sarah and Hagar placed in a primitive society, or Tolstoy's fable of the three old men who walked on the water, or Dickens' melodramas, and read them with the same absorbed attention. The primitive Semitic folklore of two thousand years ago, Tolstoy's miracles, Dickens' fantasies of lost heirs and mysterious crimes, do not make us say 'But all this is false and silly', any more than we say of a Chinese pagoda or the Taj Mahal 'What fantastic stuff'. We know that the building is there to give us a certain experience of beauty, and so we know that the book is there to give us a certain experience of moral beings in action. As we say of a building 'It is strange but all the same it is beautiful', feeling the revelation of a new formal beauty in this unexpected thing, so we say of a book 'These people and their ways are new to us but they are true', and recognise a new dimension of the moral real.

Read, for instance, that masterpiece, *The Tale of Genji*. It was written by a court lady of Japan, the Lady Murasaki, about the year 1000. It deals with a highly sophisticated society, in a civilisation quite new to us. Great noblemen write to each other in verse. It is a disgrace to have an ugly handwriting. The religion is Buddhist. Yet we are struck at every page with the truth, the revelation of the action. We see an aristocracy far more refined in a court far cleaner than that of Louis XIV.

That is to say, we recognise fundamental human nature at work in this new setting. We are continually led beyond what we know already of that nature in other settings to see how it would act in this. We pass beyond the concept of what people are like and how they can act into a new realisation of the possibilities of their nature and their action. We delight, not only in knowing these exquisite beings, but in perceiving new reaches of truth within the real. We are enlarged as well as transported.

This truth, this revelation is given to us because, for a time, we have lived with these Japanese nobles in their own world. No description, no concept could begin to do that for us. What we know of them we know by experience. And when we say of some action 'That was right', 'That was nobly done', or 'That was wrong', we are making our own judgment of a unique situation. We do not discover the meaning of this world as a concept, but as a form of moral experience. And this is the vital quality of the novelist's art, by which he gives us intuition into the real.

This can be seen at once if we consider some technical failures. Nothing is so illuminating as a great writer's mistakes, and all of them make mistakes, for all of them are struggling to express an intuition of life which transcends any possible symbolic form. All feel the limitations of language, of technique, and continually try to surpass them— like James Joyce who, in *Finnegans Wake*, finally invented a new language, but came upon the new difficulty that, though he had found a new expressive form, he had no public ready trained to understand

152

it. Yet it is beginning to be understood and, in time, will be common reading. For it comes from and goes to universal qualities of men and their preoccupations. Its difference is in its particular form, in Joyce's characteristic intuition.

But just as James Joyce and Lawrence had their characteristic intuitions of the real, so does any reader. It is, like theirs, a conditioned intuition. The reader's sensibility has acquired by education a coherent rational interest, which naturally tends to discover in daily actual experience the events that illustrate and confirm it, which is the equivalent of the writer's theme. It gives life and meaning for him. This is both his strength and his limitation. His meaning excludes other meanings. Life offers different revelations to a French catholic and an English protestant, even to a European catholic and an American one. No dogmatic schema, however elaborate, can begin to classify the exuberance of actual events for a standard valuation. But the two catholics, even the protestant and the catholic, can understand each other and say 'We see that such and such an event is important for you, only we give greater weight to this other'.

At a certain primitive level, all men agree. The Australian blackfellow and the university professor still find a common good in morality. Courage, duty, affection, loyalty, self-discipline, truth, these are fundamental values for both of them. They differ only about their relative importance.

This moral constant is of course the reason not only why the most foreign and ancient works of art from the paleolithic cave-drawings to negro carving have meaning for us but why we can enter into the moral atmosphere of societies quite strange to our own experience. For all exist and must exist within a universal moral real.

We know their truth, we can intuit the facts in the actuality of our daily life. We check our fiction by our own direct knowledge. That is to say, we can check the fundamental presentation of moral character—what we get from the author is its development, its action in his own special world. This is where we find illumination and realise a meaning for existence, a form of achievement, whether it be in the renunciation of the old aristocrat in *The Tale of Genji*, when he becomes a monk, or in the triumphant dignity of the Spartans, combing their hair at Thermopylae before certain death.

XXXIII

MEANING AND MORALITY

THE story gives the meaning, the morality. Why then does the Morality, called by that name, so hopelessly fail to convey anything of value? Take *Everyman*, where the hero, Everyman, threatened by Death, first asks Fellowship for help, and Fellowship deserts him. Then he goes to Kindred, and Kindred also backs out. At last he falls back on Good Deeds, who finally saves him from Hell.

At first sight, the failure of *Everyman* is a defect of characterisation. How are we to take any interest in such lay figures as Good Deeds and Kindred? But we don't object to Christian and Faithful, Byends or Giant Sloth in *Pilgrim's Progress*, or to Sir Wilfull by Congreve. These are like real people subject to mood and whims, but the characters of *Everyman* are mere conceptions, entirely abstract. What is more, the meaning is given in the form of a general precept, equally abstract. No real problem is proposed or answered. The whole matter could be equally well expressed in a copybook maxim. And we do not believe, really believe, copybook maxims. If we did they would simply produce confusion in our minds and conduct. We see that confusion every day in the conduct of people who do live by the maxim, the slogan, whether political, artistic or religious. They are the ideologues who force all history to fit some preconceived dialectic or blueprint, who see religion as a trick to keep the poor quiet or, alternatively, accept the miseries of poverty as ordained by God. They are people who have lost all contact with reality, who live in a fantastic world, and sooner or later they run head-first into reality and it breaks them.

The reality which smashes every ideologue and his system is human nature, incessantly striving towards a personal achievement in a world which is essentially free and personal. For the actual world does not show the consistency of a machine, which is a repetition; on the contrary, nothing in the world of actual forms is ever repeated, not even the shape of a tree. Every event, like every individual, is unique, so that the persistence of nature, as a whole, is not that of a mechanism, but of a living character, whose real existence is the only limitation upon its freedom. To exist, at all, requires a personal elemental force, but within this form there is an infinite variety of particular variation. A beech can take any shape so long as it remains a beech.

This scheme of things is, of course, offered only as a bare working point. It necessarily takes the form of a map for use. Maps use the most limited kind of symbols. Great cities are dots, rivers and roads are lines, mountains are like chicken feathers, forests are like bubbles in soda water. Cambridge and Oxford are so many miles apart and precisely the same size and shape. All the same, a map is essential to every traveller, and gives him a truth he can find nowhere else. It tells him where he is and which way he must turn to get to his destination. And a mistake in a map may completely frustrate him. When I first went to Borgu, in West Africa, I was given a map which was completely wrong. As a result I marched a hundred and fifty men and carriers twenty miles through the bush to a town that didn't exist and never had existed. We found ourselves with tired carriers and no food or water for them. The first thing I had to do in that country was to make a map. I believe that my map of Borgu is still current in the atlases—it is my proudest work. But its symbolism, in the rough bush of that remote African district, is precisely the same as that for Kent or Sussex. And must be so, to give the truth.

So my description of the real world as a character which, for us, is essentially a personal free character, is expressed only as a map to be tested by practical use and experience. And we can say at once that, though the actual worlds of Homer, of the Lady Murasaki and our own are enormously different, they present one common factor, they give us people who are free moral agents deciding their own actions in a world of inccssant vicissitude, a world as far as possible removed from the consistency of a machine, a world in which every moral problem is itself unique, in which the law courts spend millions of money and years of time assessing separately each individual charge. It is the fact of personal freedom and uniqueness in the individual soul that makes Homer and Murasaki still significant to us, or, as we say, real. Given that world of free responsible action, we can accept and comprehend the most novel and unexpected background and motive; without it, we can't accept our own Everyman in our own Europe.

This point may seem obvious, but its significance is overlooked, both for art and reality. That is why

I want to examine its force in the realm of intuitive realisation, the subconscious of the reader.

I said that all artists are concerned to give meaning to the actual, and that for writers the actuality is that of human society, of individuals working out their own destinies.

All writers have, and must have, to compose any kind of story, some picture of the world, and of what is right and wrong in that world. And the great writers are obsessed with their theme. They're sure they're right, and their message would save the world. This is as true of Lawrence as of Tolstoy, or Dante, or the monkish author of *Everyman*.

It is just because this monk was so sure of his meaning that he wrote allegory. Allegory is the most certain method of giving a clear and exact meaning. What could be clearer than the message, the meaning of Everyman?

Just because of this clearness, this definition of meaning, allegory is a standing temptation to the great writers. What's more, their greatest triumphs are achieved in that narrow space between allegory and the dramatic scene. Lawrence's masterpiece, *St Mawr*, is an example. The stallion, St Mawr, represents the uncorrupted male energy, instinctive, free from all conceptual whims, entirely real. The scene where it throws and nearly kills Rico Carrington is very close to allegory. For Rico represents the intellectualism of culture which Lawrence hated as a decadence, as the conceptual enemy of the intuitive real. He makes his point. We may think Lawrence's theme too narrow for its development. It was itself, of course, the product of an intellectual who built upon his single intuition an immense conceptual structure covering every kind of human relation and even political theory. But the intuition was true and profound. Lawrence is a great writer because he had a true intuition and devised the technical means of making us realise it for ourselves. He made us know and remember a vital truth that is easy to forget. And in spite of the fact that St Mawr and Rico Carrington are designed to represent generalities quite as wide as Everyman and Good Deeds, we realise Lawrence's truth in this sense of violence. We are not frustrated by any suspicion of allegory. St Mawr, for all its representative character, remains the stallion and Rico Carrington, the poor fish, all manner and talk and no real quality of faith, of purpose, of feeling, the hollow figment of a man.

Lawrence has got his effect with almost the precision of allegory, but without falling into that trap. But compare this scene in *St Mawr* with that in Tolstoy's *Anna Karenina* between Vronsky and the English mare. The mare falls in the race owing, as Tolstoy tells us, to an awkward movement by Vronsky. This breaks her back. She lies there, unable to get up. Vronsky kicks her in his fury and she struggles to obey him. We are checked at once so that we stop and look again and ask, 'Is this

Vronsky and the mare or an allegory of Vronsky and Anna, of Tolstoy's society male and his unhappy female? Is it a puppet show, with Tolstoy pulling the strings?'

To the critical judgment Tolstoy ought to be on far safer ground than Lawrence. Vronsky, no doubt, is a typical soldier, but much more individual in character, much less of a representative type than Carrington. What adds to Vronsky's independence as an individual is that he is given to us among half-a-dozen other guards officers, all typical soldiers, but all sharply differentiated. And the English mare has been established for us simply as a thoroughbred without any representative character at all such as Lawrence has imposed on St Mawr.

Why, then, does Tolstoy, infinitely a greater artist than Lawrence, cause us so much uneasiness in the actual reading, whereas Lawrence succeeds so completely in a scene even more charged with symbolic significance? Why, that is, does an episode which to the critical judgment is soundly contrived have so ruinous an effect in the actual experience of the reader? Why does this scene suddenly become allegorical when Lawrence's escaped free?

For one thing, we see at once a parallel between the mare's relation with Vronsky, and Anna's, both at his mercy. And there is no such parallel suggested in St Mawr.

XXXIV

MEANS AND ENDS

TOLSTOY is a master of form and *Anna Karenina* was his masterpiece in formal perfection. How was he tempted into allegory? The professional answer is that he was haunted by his theme. Necessarily so. It was his form, and *Anna Karenina* is a masterpiece because every detail belongs to the formal unity of Tolstoy's meaning. Here he had organised a race meeting, to bring all his characters in play. And it takes no less than ten chapters. It's true that all these chapters carry the story forward and illustrate the theme. They show us the relations between the husband, Alexei and Anna, and between Anna and Vronsky in a new development. Anna's agitation when she sees Vronsky's fall during the race produces the critical interview with her husband when she declares that she hates him. All the same, this long succession of scenes has a certain monotony, and we know from Tolstoy's diary that this is exactly what he dreaded at this part of the book. He may well have thought that the race itself, which is the ostensible excuse for the whole ten chapters, would be an anti-climax unless it provided some dramatic peak, some new light upon the theme. So he builds up the dramatic climax of the race as an allegory of Vronsky's relations with Anna and a premonition of her fate when she too is physically unable to serve his will.

He does not make it too obvious an allegory. He realises for us all the details with his usual marvellous skill—the mare, the trainer, the whole racing background are from actual life, so is the race. And he hopes, no doubt, that we shall be carried along by our delighted sense of this brilliant art with such force that we will accept the intrusion of a conceptual idea without noticing its falseness. We will simply feel it subconsciously, in horrified sympathy for the innocent mare, as a vague but strong sense of the tragic relations between the wilful impatient egotism of the man and the patient feminine devotion of his victim. But unluckily our critical mind jumps up at once. We feel uneasy probably for the very reason that Tolstoy has succeeded in giving us the emotional effect that he intended—but an effect not congruent with the situation of the moment, involving characters we have accepted as actual in an actual world. We are checked by a false note.

Perhaps we are already uneasy. We have heard much of Vronsky's love of this mare, of her beauty, her high breeding. Tolstoy describes her as a creature so sensitive that we wonder she can't speak. Now we see her lying at his feet, she bends her head back and gazes at him with her speaking eyes. The very suspicion of allegory destroys the validity of the scene. Suddenly the characters become mere concepts invented to illustrate a theme, and the theme itself a precept out of a copybook.

Allegory is an immense temptation to the writer,

especially the great, the obsessed writer. As we have seen, his problem is to translate his intuition into concept and his concept back into a vehicle which conveys the intuition. Allegory gives a clear, a definite meaning; not to the soul, but to the conceptual judgment, and in a form of dry precept whose falsity is at once detected by the soul. For that soul does not live in a world of pedagogues laying down general laws, but in the free world of persons whose feelings are individual and whose actions are always particular. To say honesty is the best policy is nonsense to a mother whose child is a fool. She knows that it would be fatal to say to that child 'You're a fool and it's no good your trying', for it will make the child either miserable as well as stupid, or defiant and revengeful. She encourages the child. She says 'Don't worry about your reports. You'll come on later. When you're older, you'll learn quite easily.' In fact, she is far from honest, she uses untruth to avoid a worse evil, and to bring a good end. This is true of all such problems. It is not even true that the end justifies the means. The question in real life is what means, and what ends? What is the particular situation we're talking about? Allegory is false because it lays down categorical imperatives for conduct in a world of particular and unique events. It treats the world as a mechanism whereas it is a world of free souls. And it is in this world of persons that the novelist must develop his meanings. He must show his meaning by creating persons who have

163

the character of actual persons, in a world that could be actual but displays a moral order that does not present itself in life. It is an ideal order which remains an object of attainment for that writer in the world as he knows it in fact.

It is by experience of these ordered worlds that the reader, who needs such an idea for himself in his own world, is enriched. Reading is not only a keen pleasure to the senses and judgment, it brings to the imagination a special enlargement, a special knowledge. It is like foreign travel. The man who goes to Africa or India finds whole peoples living under different laws, a different religion, a different social idea, different arts, and sees that under these conditions they achieve themselves in their own way. Yet they are essentially the same kind of people as himself. Such a discovery is a prophylactic against narrow minds, unless, of course, the traveller goes out with a mind made up that his own national customs and prejudices are the only right ones. This, however, is a common enough phenomenon, especially among those modern travellers who move only in groups of fellow countrymen. They support each other's prejudices and protect each other against any experience that might break through the conceptual blindness of a national ego.

For the gap between experience and thought, direct knowledge of the real and the reflective judgment, can be bridged in the subconscious, but only by the symbol which is highly fragile and very easily breaks down. We saw how allegory can break it, instantly dividing the reader into an emotional memory which is already losing significance, and a conceptual judgment which is coldly analysing and labelling a set of technical tricks.

We know how many people go about the world precisely in this condition—men who are on the one hand emotional without sense and on the other full of the most rigid opinions on every possible subject without regard either to fact or sensibility. It has been said that after twenty-five, few people are open to new ideas on any subject—they are crusted over with a conceptual education which has entirely cut them off from the living world.

The concept, the label, is perpetually hiding from us all the nature of the real. We have to have conceptual knowledge to organise our societies, to save our own lives, to lay down general ends for conduct, to engage in any activity at all, but that knowledge, like the walls we put up to keep out the weather, shuts out the real world and the sky. It is a narrow little house which becomes a prison to those who can't get out of it.

The artist, the writer, simply in order to give his realisation, his truth, has to break these walls, the conceptual crust. His meaning is aimed at the whole character of the man, his soul. As we saw, this is one reason why certain artists, certain writers, invent new symbolic systems. They are so deeply aware of the crust of a received convention and of the weakness of run-down symbols which have lost all their dynamic energy, that they invent new ones, charged with their own explosive power.

XXXV

THE FORM OF ALLEGORY

THIS matter of allegory may seem too unimportant to be treated at such length. But it is not so. We are asking how does a great writer overcome all the obstacles of conceptual judgment and the deceitful symbol to give us a truth about reality in the only way it can be given—to make us feel it. He is bound, like all of us, by the doom of freedom which gives us both all the tragedy and all the joy of life, to use the symbol. He has to create the work of art, by hard conceptual labour, and yet to convey an ordered whole of feeling. He has no other means of expressing his meaning, his intuition to other free and separate souls. And it is only by examining actual works of art that we can find out something about the difficulties.

It is easy to see that Lawrence's *St Mawr*, so close to allegory, is a triumph, but why does Tolstoy, a far greater artist than Lawrence, fail? Where is his miscalculation? I suggest simply in a forgetfulness of character. Vronsky's rage startles us, and always seems to me untrue to that well-disciplined guardsman. And the mare is made to act out of character.

This is an important and interesting point. For the mare is true to her own character, to horse character. I have myself had such a horse, with the same sensibility, the same loyalty. But in the story, she is suddenly made to represent the feminine principle as Tolstoy conceived it.

A character in a story is part of the meaning. Anna is representative of womanhood and we accept her as a real woman, in Tolstoy's sense. Because she is true also to our sense. We would accept women as women that Tolstoy would describe as unwomanly. We have a wider idea of what women can do in the world and still be essentially women, good wives, good mothers. But Tolstoy has not raised any such larger questions. He has given us a woman who is woman to us as well as to him, at once a living individual and a typical woman.

The mare is a real mare, but we have not received her as representative of the feminine character in the book. She appears simply as a part of the background of Vronsky's life which, for Tolstoy, represents the artificial structure of that high society in which Anna is corrupted. His sudden change of meaning is a false note. I use the word deliberately. For the effect is analogous to that of the false note in music which interrupts suddenly the recreation of the structure of our subconscious and causes our critical judgment to start up and say 'What's happened—what's wrong?'

And what's wrong in this case is simply that the

meaning of a note, or phrase, the mare, has been forced into a context that doesn't belong to it. So she loses even her own character as a mare—she becomes like a performing animal, a puppet, manipulated by Tolstoy. St Mawr is not a puppet because his meaning in the tale is not only one with his nature, but with his function in the tale.

For we must remember always a tale is not life, it is art and subject to the limitations of art, in this case, to the logic of the subconscious, allotting by association a meaning to each character, to each development, in a construction that is fundamentally As If.

But As If itself is a temptation. Look at Hardy's *Tess of the d'Urbervilles*, where Tess, having murdered her seducer, the man who has destroyed her life, is escaping from the police. She is lost in the fog on Salisbury Plain, and worn out at last, while the police close in, she lies down on the only dry spot, a flat stone. As the fog lifts, this stone is found to be the altar stone in Stonehenge, and Hardy writes of it as the stone of sacrifice.

She ceases, that is, to be Tess involved in her personal tragedy. She has become a figment, a stage property. Yet Hardy is among the very greatest. The more we recede from him in time, the greater he seems, like Wordsworth's mountain. He is master, like Shakespeare, of the great dramatic scene. But it is this very mastery that has betrayed him to this disastrous scene on the stone of sacrifice. Or perhaps I should say that it is his intense intuition of the injustice, the uncertainty, the blind cruelty of fate, that drove him to use so crude an allegory. Like Lawrence, he cannot bear the complacency, the self-satisfaction of the world. He wants to get under the skin of this pachyderm. And he has forgotten for the moment that the artist has no weapon that will penetrate the most delicate material carcass. He deals with the persons, with the souls, with the ghost in the machine. He must catch it when it is not aware of itself as a mind, a person, or character, when it has no practical aim or will, and when it has taken off the armour of its conceptual judgment, its conventional ideas, the tension of fear and hate, in order to relax. In this state it does not want to hear sermons; nine times in ten it does not want to learn anything at all, it wants only enjoyment, self-forgetfulness. And he must give it—the dream. He must transport this lounger into another existence, and make him know what he wants him to know, as an experience, as a realisation that simply happens to him. So when a passing headlight shows a landscape both unexpected and familiar, it is not for a long time that this glimpse reveals itself to him as an important event.

It is Hardy, who, more than anyone, has devised such scenes of which we can hardly put the meaning into words, and, like Shakespeàre, he goes to great lengths to contrive them. In *The Mayor of Casterbridge*, we have Henchard, ruined, going to commit suicide. As he looks over the bridge at the mill-pool, he sees his own corpse turning in the current. To bring this about Hardy has had to invent the Skimmington riders who carry Henchard's effigy in procession, and the police who catch them, so that they throw their guy into the river. He has asked us to accept an elaborate coincidence of event, time and place. But we accept it without difficulty as we accept the elaborate scenes in Joyce's *Ulysses*, or the miracles of Tolstoy's fables. We are not critical of material fact in this dream world, but only of meanings. What does this incident mean for us, and for Henchard? It shocks us into an intuition, through Henchard's intuition, of death, not as a word, a common idea, but as it is in reality, an ever-present threat, an ultimate fact. For in the real world our death is always with us. That is why de Rancé, Abbot of La Trappe, slept in his coffin, to have the experience, renewed every day, of truth, to break the crust of the conceptual world.

The churches use all the arts—architecture, rhetoric, music, drama, poetry—to give us back only one single piece of real knowledge, the experience of goodness, of the good man, as an ultimate fact, something we cannot dodge, and something that, when we know it, changes the whole nature of things for our feeling, and gives a new meaning to our world.

Hardy, again in *Tess*, accomplishes this for us. The scene again not only renews for us a final truth, but throws light on the means by which a great art achieves its ends. If you remember, Tess is the poor farm girl of a family actually descended from the great Norman family of d'Urberville. The parson of the Parish tells them of their descent and they think to make something of it by sending Tess, who is a pretty girl, to call cousin with some rich people called d'Urberville in the neighbourhood. These d'Urbervilles are actually nothing of the sort, they have assumed the name for snob reasons. They do give Tess work in the yard, and the son of the house promptly seduces her, and she returns home to have her baby. Her parents, easy-going and feckless throughout, accept this misfortune with cheerful resignation; but Tess is very much ashamed, and, when the baby is born, she doesn't take it to be christened. She hides it and herself away from the public eye, but the baby pines. One night she is afraid it will die, and she says 'What a wicked girl I am. I have brought this poor little thing into the world without any father to look after it, and now, if it dies, it will go to Hell because of my cowardice. But,' she says, 'perhaps God will forgive it if it has some kind of a christening.' So she gets her little brothers and sisters out of bed to act as congregation, and takes her prayer-book, and christens the baby in the wash-basin.

This is a very powerful and moving scene, and one asks why it has such force. Hardy takes that oldest relation of mother and child and gives it a new aspect for us. He shows Tess as responsible for the child's soul, and he shows it in a dramatic form. He renews for us also the christening service, because it is Tess, the mother, with all her obsessive anxiety for that child's salvation, who performs it. He adds to the dramatic intensity of the situation all the weight of dramatic ritual as it lies in our recollection. Thus the scene, acquiring a monumental character, is contrasted with the simplicity of the background, and it never loses its power and significance for us.

XXXVI

POWER OF THE SYMBOL

WHAT is commoner than mother-love? It is a platitude, vulgarised, a joke in the music-halls. It is, as symbol, such a bore that the modern fashion, at least among writers who are afraid to deal with a fundamental real because it seems to them too ordinary, too trite, who seek not the new expression but some new concept, is to represent it as an evil. But Hardy, as a great writer, deals only with great and simple issues. He breaks through the conceptual and habitual crust of everyday, where every activity has its common use and its conceptual label, where life wears the mask of a mechanical pursuit of material aims, of temporal appeasement, and reveals to us what we had forgotten, that what makes life worth living are

such common things as family love, ordinary goodness and truth, the duty and self-sacrifice which we
know every day in the smallest as well as the greatest
actions.

This the great artist accomplishes by manipulation
of the symbol, with all its defects. It is the only
means available to him. On the other hand, I suggest
that the essential power of the symbol resides in
these very defects. For, as we have seen, its weakness is in its failure to be exact either as label, as
concept—because it carries invariably association of
feeling—or as consistent vehicle of emotion—because it is always sinking back into a mere sign. But
since, however unstable, it combines both elements, it
is the only means by which it is possible to achieve any
unity between the knowledge of fact and the feeling
about the fact, the machine and the soul, the universal consistencies and the individual character, so
that they can be joined together in an ordered
experience of the real which, we must suppose,
includes them both in one total personal character
of existence.

We suppose so, but we can't prove it. Our sup-
position is, in fact, conceptual, but so far as it is
based on an intuition of beauty and goodness in
nature, it has great force. We say 'If nature has
meaning for us as beauty, it cannot be alien to our
soul, which recognises that beauty and delights in
it. For beauty is not only a feeling, it is also a relation.
If every born child has power to love, then goodness

is a natural thing, as natural as hydrogen gas, and we belong to a world of personal value.' All men, whatever they may think they believe, live in this faith. Their particular difference is in their reaction to it, the use they make of it in pursuit of some personal achievement, good or bad. They do not escape from reality even while as mechanists or positivists they deny any meaning to its values. Denial is easy because of the independence of the mind and its imagination, capable of any fantasy and able, by the force of ideas, to impose an order of habitual reaction upon the feelings.

But such education of the whole man again can be carried out only by means of the charged symbol, at once concept and experience. It is the ambivalence of the symbol that enables the artist, as teacher or expositor, as creator of meanings, to bridge the gap between the individual idea and the universal real of emotion, forming by art a personality which unites them both in a single active and rational will. That character may be fantastic, evil or mad, according to the form laid upon the complex of personal feeling, it may also be true in the sense that it does not necessarily come into conflict with any part of the material and moral real, that it enables a man to live with truth.

This is the only real truth that we can know, and art is the only means by which we can achieve it. It is only in great art and the logic of the subconscious where judgment has become part of the individual emotional character that we move freely in a world which is at once concept and feeling, rational order and common emotion, in a dream which is truer than actual life and a reality which is only there made actual, complete and purposeful to our experience.